Find A Reason To Be Thankful

Olive Tetteh-Hervie

Find A Reason To Be Thankful
Copyright © 2021 by Olive Tetteh-Hervie

All rights reserved. No part of this publication may be reproduced, distributed, or transmitted in any form or by any means, including photocopying, recording, or other electronic or mechanical methods, without the prior written permission of the author, except in the case of brief quotations embodied in critical reviews and certain other non-commercial uses permitted by copyright law.

Tellwell Talent
www.tellwell.ca

ISBN
978-0-2288-6641-1 (Paperback)
978-0-2288-6642-8 (eBook)

All rights reserved. No part of this publication may be reproduced, stored in a retrieval system or transmitted in any form or by any means—for example, electronic, photocopy, recording—without the prior written permission of the author. The only exception is brief quotations in reviews or for Christian ministry purposes.

Unless otherwise noted, all Scriptures are taken from The Holy Bible, New King James Version®. Copyright © 1982 by Thomas Nelson, Inc. All rights reserved.

Scriptures marked (NIV) are taken from The Holy Bible, New International Version® NIV® Copyright © 1973, 1978, 1984 by International Bible Society® Used by permission. All rights reserved worldwide.

Scriptures marked Easy-to-Read Version are taken from The Holy Bible: Easy-to-Read Version. Copyright © 2001 by World Bible Translation Center. All rights reserved.

Published in Canada (2021)

Contact: reasontobethankful@gmail.com

Table of Contents

DEDICATION..vii
APPRECIATION ix
FOREWORD xi
INTRODUCTION
Chapter 1: WHY THANKFULNESS 1
Chapter 2: COUNT YOUR BLESSINGS 23
Chapter 3: SMILE 43
Chapter 4: APPRECIATE NATURE..52
Chapter 5: HOW ABOUT YOUR TALENT?..............................65
Chapter 6: LOOK OUT FOR THE GOOD IN OTHERS............77
Chapter 7: DO NOT COMPARE YOURSELF TO OTHERS.... 85
Chapter 8: PRACTICE THANKFULNESS............................... 96

APPENDIX.. 107
PRAYER 109
WORKS CITED.. 111

DEDICATION

I would like to dedicate this book to God Almighty who knew me before I was formed in my mother's womb and chose me to be part of His great Kingdom.

I also dedicate this book to my mother who despite the stressful situation she found herself in (as she was not married then) stuck to the fear of abortion, ignored all odds and gave birth to me. Her consolation was in Hebrews 13:2 *Do not forget to entertain strangers, for by so doing some have unwittingly entertained angels.* Thank God it paid off.

I encourage anyone reading this who may find themselves in a similar situation as my mom to please take a moment and think of what your unborn baby could become. I tell you, those children could become the greatest blessings to mankind.

APPRECIATION

I am thankful to the Holy Spirit, my teacher and my helper, who instructs me on what to do.

I am thankful for Wailing Women Worldwide, Women Intercessors for the Church and the Nations, who have given me the opportunity to exercise my ministry gifting as I continue to mature in the Lord.

My heartfelt gratitude to my family and friends who saw potential in me and encouraged me to rise to my calling.

Finally, I am grateful to my children for their love and support and to Jonas, my husband and mentor, who prayed for me to know the Lord and has walked with me on my journey of faith. To God be the glory.

FOREWORD

These days, the term "woman of faith" is used as a description for any Christian woman. The expression has lost its substance and value. In the Bible, faith took a risk on God. It stood out and did not follow the crowd. Abraham trusted God with his future, his life and the lives of those with him when he followed God out of his native country of Ur. He earned the title "Father of Faith." It is by the biblical definition of faith that I introduce Olive Tetteh-Hervie, a woman of faith and the author of *Find a Reason to Be Thankful*.

Faith in and obedience to the Word of God is Olive Tetteh-Hervie's lifestyle. From seemingly smaller things like the fixing of her car to greater things like the supernatural healing of a loved one, I have seen her stand by God's Word. For as long as I've known Olive, her trust is in God for every situation. She has been a practical example to me and to others as someone who trusts in His faithfulness for every detail of her life. I thank God often for her. In fact, I believe she is the answer to one of my prayers. One night, as a young Christian, I looked up to the sky and cried out to the Lord, asking Him where the true Christians were. Where were the men and women like those in the book of Acts? It was not long after that He led me to a church where I met Olive.

Since I met her in 2013 and until now, I have known her as a mentor, a co-worker in the Kingdom of God, and as a sister. As a committed intercessor in Wailing Women Worldwide (WWW), she has a dual role as a National and Provincial Coordinator and leads Canada's Worship and the Facilitators' team in WWW. Olive Tetteh-Hervie's life is dedicated to the work of God and His Kingdom.

It was in obedience to the Lord that this woman of faith wrote *Find a Reason to Be Thankful*. God's timing is on time. Today, thankfulness has a connotation of being a nicety; it's a small gesture that is embraced in our society; it's something that is said. However, just as the expression "woman of faith" has depreciated, so too has thankfulness. Throughout church history, revelations are forgotten and found again. This book unearths the transformative power and blessings that thankfulness releases when practiced in our daily lives. It also equips us with a defence for the time that we are living. In 2 Timothy, Paul warns us that the last days will be dangerous times of great stress and trouble, and one of the reasons is because people will be unthankful (3:1–2). This book brings both blessings and protection to those who read it.

It is the truth when I say that I enjoyed and benefited from reading the chapters of this book over and over. There is life in this book and life will prove itself. My prayer as we read *Find a Reason to Be Thankful* is that we will not forget all that the Lord shows us and teaches us. May He transform us and reveal to us the true meaning of thankfulness, for being thankful is the will of God for our lives (1 Thessalonians 5:18).

Julie Russell
National Coordinator for Wailing Women Worldwide Canada

***

This book is a true reality check and a timely reminder not to take anything for granted. It is an easy read for all; it encourages those who are already very thankful to be consistent while challenging everyone to begin a lifestyle of thanksgiving. The author of *Find a Reason to Be Thankful,* Olive Tetteh-Hervie, is a close friend and co-labourer in God's Vineyard, and she actively lives what she has written in this book. For me, this life of gratitude completely transformed my perspective and opened my eyes to see what God was already doing in my life. I wholeheartedly recommend this book and I pray earnestly that it will bring a lasting change in attitude and mindset for all who will read it.

Uche Ezechim
Ontario Certified Teacher (OCT)
Author of *The Fruitful Vine and Olive Shoots.*
American Continental Coordinator for Wailing Women Worldwide

***

    This book, *Find a Reason to Be Thankful,* is a reminder to everyone, both Christian and non-Christian, to reflect upon their daily lives. Indeed, when you ponder on how you have overcome many of life's challenges that overwhelmed you, yet you survived them in ways that surprised you, then you will understand that there is a greater force working behind the veil to help you. It is the divine force—the God-factor. Ironically, many people do not reckon with it. The reason is that they do not understand it. Indeed, this book is a call to think better and thank better. God is always behind the veil working for us, and for this we must be thankful. Many of us complain about the things that are yet to be accomplished instead of being grateful for the accomplished. The author of this book is challenging us to always be thankful.

    This book could not have been written by a better author. I have known the author, Olive Tetteh-Hervie for six years now as a very strong personality, full of passion and resilience. She is an ardent follower of Christ and speaks and writes directly from her heart. This piece comes to us in a time when many have lost their sense of gratitude and thankfulness. It teaches the reader of the imperative to be grateful for those things God does for His people that we tend to overlook. I wholeheartedly agree with the views she has expressed here, and I do not hesitate to recommend it to anyone who wants to experience the efficacy of thankfulness. I believe this book in our hands will attract the blessings of God, for when we learn to be thankful, then we open the doors for greater blessings.

Regina Nwachukwu
Lead National Coordinator for Wailing Women Worldwide Canada
Early Childhood Educator

***

Very few people realize the importance of thanksgiving and appreciation. People are so preoccupied with the things they do not have that they can hardly behold what they do have in hand. This is true even among some Christians.

The prayer lists of many are filled with requests upon requests and almost void of appreciation to GOD for the many things HE does for us, especially for giving us life.

I therefore commend the author for being like the one leper, not being more occupied with her problems and solutions but with the One who made her and has solutions to every possible problem she may face.

She didn't stop at expressing her appreciation, but saw it fit to encourage and remind her readers today and years to come that thanksgiving is essential. If we follow this example, we can better enjoy the blessings we receive.

Rev. Dr. Mrs. Joyce Frimpong
Assemblies of God, Jehovah Jireh Temple
Author of *Rare Reflections*

***

We are in a season of thanksgiving, but the devil is strategically changing it into a season of worry, fear and complaints. The author of this book, who is also my oldest sister, is spreading the good news of thanksgiving through this book to remind us as believers and nonbelievers to strategically choose to be thankful to God everyday. As a registered nurse, I am constantly reminded to be thankful. You can successfully overcome complaints by counting all your blessings and you will have so much to be grateful for. *Find a Reason to Be Thankful,* for a thankful heart honours God. Let's be joyful and thankful in all circumstances for this is what the Lord wants from us in our union with Christ Jesus. 1 Thessalonians

Gloria Nti-Addae, RN
Prayer Leader, Agape Unlimited Church

INTRODUCTION

We are living in an era where complaining is the order of the day. Of course, there are many things going wrong and things seem to be deteriorating by the day. However, this should not come as a surprise because the Bible makes it clear that these are the signs of the end times. The Bible has been redefined to suit men's lust to the extent that even morality has been distorted. These stem out of dissatisfaction and greed and that is why men are **UNTHANKFUL**.

Unfortunately, even believers who profess faith in Christ Jesus have slowly been drawn into this attitude of complaining without being conscious of it. Things around us have become sometimes overwhelmingly unbearable with the pressures of life and also spiritual battles.

This presents the inevitable question: *Is there anything to be thankful for when things seem to be spinning out of control?* Yes, there is because God has not changed. His faithfulness to mankind and to His children remains steadfast. This gives us a reason to be thankful. God's faithfulness through Jesus Christ is what sustains us in trying times. Thankfulness has the power to change an atmosphere of hopelessness to hope. It has the power to bring the presence of God into any situation. Thankfulness is our response to faith in the Word of God.

It is my prayer that this book will encourage you to be the light in the darkness by starting conversations on thanksgiving to light up the world.

Olive Tetteh-Hervie

Chapter 1

WHY THANKFULNESS

Thankfulness is an expression of gratitude. For thanksgiving to be meaningful, there must be a reason for it. Thanksgiving is usually expressed in response to a service rendered, a gift or an expression of kindness.

It is very common to hear "thank you" at least once a day when you are interacting with people. This could be in spoken or written form or even through sign language. In fact, thanksgiving is part and parcel of daily living. As common as thanksgiving is, its impact is experienced when it comes from a genuine heart.

God created man in His image, and He expects thanksgiving from man in the same way man expects thanksgiving from a fellow man. When we fail or neglect to give thanks, it is detrimental not only to ourselves but also to those to whom we owe gratitude. It reflects a lack of appreciation and robs us of the joy that is meant to be ours and for those around us. God commands us through His word to be thankful because a thankful person is a grateful person. Thankfulness is a biblical imperative.

Psalm 107:1 *Oh, give thanks to the Lord, for He is good! For His mercy endures forever.*

We have an obligation to give thanks to God because He is good. The Bible indicates that every good and perfect gift comes from God. Each day we are blessed to experience anything good in our lives—good health, family, friends, food, clean water, etc. We should acknowledge that God gives them to us, and we ought to be thankful to Him.

Each day of my life, I make it a point to mention most or all these good things listed above in a prayer of thanksgiving to God. I have realized that sometimes when the things we take for granted stop working the way they should, it is then that some of us appreciate that everything we have is a gift from God. For example, if I wake up one morning, and turn my water tap on only to discover that there is no running water (after enjoying running water without any interruptions for years), I suddenly begin to appreciate how blessed I am. We do not have to wait to experience shortage before we learn to appreciate God for even the little things.

Consider the fact that when we close our eyes to sleep, we never know exactly when we drift off. We can only say we slept around a certain time but exactly when we became partly conscious in sleep is not something we know. Do you know that sleep is a gift from God? There were months in my life that I was sleeping very little for no apparent reason. Then one day I went to church, and there was a word of knowledge that came, saying that some people were struggling to sleep at night. I stood up along with other people and was prayed for. Since that time, I have slept like a baby. We should not take it for granted when we are able to sleep without interruption and without the help of pills. We should remember each morning that though our alarms may sound, if God our creator does not wake us up, we can never open our eyes to see the light of day. Therefore, let us learn to count every blessing and name them before God, and tell Him how appreciative we are for what He has done for us.

Whatever our minds are directed toward is what we will focus on. Therefore, if our minds are full of thanksgiving, our focus will be on the many positive things that happen every day. Such thankfulness comes with many benefits that are not always recognized.

Thankfulness is a sign of faith in God

Thanking God for what you are expecting Him to do is the strongest expression of faith in Him because it is a manifestation of what you believe.

Hebrews 11:1 *Now faith is substance of things hoped for, the evidence of things not seen.*

Ordinarily, we give thanks after we have received something. When we thank God after we have prayed, we are acknowledging that we trust Him and that we have confidence that He has already done what we have asked for. I have done this many times in my life, and anytime I have been consistent with thanksgiving after prayer, I see the manifestation of what I have asked for. Instead of going back and repeating the same prayer, I turn the request into thanksgiving and pray in the Holy Spirit until I see the manifestation of what I asked for. Of course, there are times when the Holy Spirit will show you things that are holding back the manifestation of your prayer, so you may have to do some warfare to resolve it in between; after that, you go back to thanksgiving.

1 John 5:14 *Now this is the confidence that we have in Him, that if we ask anything according to His will, He hears us.*

I believe that thanking God for what we are yet to receive helps our imagination. In the case of healing of a leg, for example, as you begin to thank Him that you can walk, you start seeing yourself walking instead of seeing yourself immobile. The moment you say aloud, "Father, I thank you that I can walk," you are calling forth the things that are not as though they were. According to Romans 4:17:

(as it is written, I have made you a father of many nations) in the presence of Him whom he believed—God, who gives life to the dead and calls those things which do not exist as though they did.

When you eventually begin walking, it will be of no surprise to you. When you start thanking God, your mind may tell you are being foolish, but once you see the manifestation of what you have been thanking God for, it becomes easier to keep practicing that. Sometimes, it may take a long time for you to see the manifestation, but thanking God will give you the strength to keep at it and not to get weary. I have seen this in my own health—from overcoming a flu to a lump disappearing from my body. Thankfulness has been a great arsenal in battling the challenges of life. You never lose when you are thanking God. Instead of declaring your current situation as it is, declare what you want to see. This does not mean you are denying what you are going through, but rather you are acknowledging God's presence and power in your situation by thanking Him (according to the Word of God).

Thanksgiving opens the door to the supernatural

The Bible is full of supernatural occurrences. The examples are innumerable. The children of Israel crossed the Red Sea as on dry ground. Daniel emerged unhurt from a den of hungry lions. The three young Hebrew men survived the flames of a blazing fiery furnace. The axe head floated after the prophet Elisha prayed. Jesus turned the water into wine and fed over five thousand people with five loaves of bread and two fish. Peter walked on water. The eyes of blind Bartimaeus were opened. The lame walked and the dead were brought back to life. These are but a few of the innumerable amazing miracles recorded in the Bible. God has already made available to us everything we would ever need in this life to have such experiences. 2 Peter 1:3 says, *His divine power has given to us all things that pertain to life and godliness, through the knowledge of Him who called us by glory and virtue.* However, we receive them by faith activated through our thanksgiving. When we thank God for what He has already done, it is an indication that we believe Him, and He is committed to doing the supernatural.

Thankfulness will result in more revelation from God

When God gives you an illumination from His word, either through a preaching or your personal Bible study, be thankful for the word and for the one who delivered the word. The more thankful you are to Him; the more revelation God will make available to you. As you thank God for your pastor or a preacher who blessed you, God will grant that person more revelation to continue to help you.

Thankfulness places you under God's favour

The dictionary meaning of favour is to prefer someone, especially in a seemingly unfair way. As a believer in Christ Jesus, it takes the favour of God to advance in this world.

Luke 2:52 *And Jesus increased in wisdom and stature, and in favour with God and man.*

If Jesus, the Son of God, needed favour on earth, then we as children of God need it too. Our thankfulness to God will cause Him to treat us in a way which may seem unfair to the world, but to Him, He is treating us with favour. You could have all the knowledge and skills in this world, but if God's favour is not upon your life, you will live a very unfulfilled life. Sometimes,

I hear people make comments about others such as "I do not know what it is, but there is something about this person which attracts me." Sometimes, you may not be the most brilliant person in a group, but favour will cause you to be noticed and utilized. Our thanksgiving will provoke the faithfulness of God.

Jerimiah 30:19 *Then out of them shall proceed thanksgiving and the voice of those who make merry; I will multiply them, and they shall not diminish; I will also glorify them, and they shall not be small.*

A grateful heart is an attractive heart. People tend to be attracted toward individuals who are thankful. In Luke 17:11–19, Jesus healed ten lepers but only one came back to express thanks. To that person He said, "Your faith has made you whole." He received wholeness in addition to healing. *And He said unto him, Arise, go thy way: thy faith hath made thee whole.* In this passage, the man was expecting healing, but he received more than that. The man was healed from leprosy, and in addition, he was made whole as though nothing happened to him.

It would not be unusual for a parent to be inclined to do more for the child who is always grateful than for the one who takes them for granted. I heard a story of a preacher who took his five-year-old child out to have fun for the day, and when he put him to bed that night, the child's last words were, "You are such a good dad." This is so touching. The preacher said he felt like picking his son out of bed and repeating the entire day. After so many years, the preacher still talks about it because his son's gratefulness left an indelible imprint on his heart.

Sometimes, the cares of this world make us focus on what we do not have rather than what we already have. We can either see the glass half empty or half full. I often pause to say, "Father, thank you that I have a job"—especially when I get paid. It may not be my dream job, but it is still a job that pays me, and I must be thankful. There are people who have a greater skillset than I do who could have done what I am doing, and could have done more, but do not have the opportunity. We must learn to be grateful. I must mention here that it should not be done just once. In the case of having a job, we should express thanksgiving to God when we first get a job and continue offering thanks to Him for it. We should keep telling Him how grateful we are for the different things He has done and is doing for us. Once we do that, He will do more and will surprise us with things we did not even ask for. When I feel overwhelmed with my workload, I speak out loud, "Father, thank you that I have a job." Once I do that, the stress leaves me.

Mary Magdalene was delivered by Jesus from evil spirits and she was one of the few who stood at the cross when Jesus was being crucified. Jesus healed and delivered many people but where were they at His crucifixion? Obviously, Mary Magdalene was one of the few very grateful followers of Jesus. It is no surprise that she was the first to see Jesus after He resurrected. That is what the expression of gratitude can do.

Being thankful prevents complaining

Ungrateful people are usually complainers. Human beings are more likely to complain than to be thankful. In fact, you cannot be thankful and complain at the same time. Paul the apostle cautions in 2 Timothy 3:1–2 *But know this, that in the last days perilous times will come: ² For men will be lovers of themselves, lovers of money, boasters, proud, blasphemers, disobedient to parents, **unthankful**, unholy.*

Being unthankful is a sign of the end times, and we are closer to the end of this age than we have ever been. Men are unthankful indeed because they never seem to be content with what they have, and that attitude of discontentment makes them unthankful. People do not seem able to enjoy a new thing before they start thinking of something else they want to get. Knowledge has increased and because of that, the rate of innovation—especially in the technological industry—is very high. There are new inventions all the time. While it is good to have the latest gadget to make us more effective in our vocations, we must be careful to take time first to be thankful for the blessings we already have.

There is an observation I have made over the years. On the days I commute to work, I realize that what starts a conversation between two strangers is usually something negative—either the train was late, or someone said or did something wrong, or they are making fun of what someone did. I hardly find people starting a conversation to appreciate the goodness of God. Even if they do, they will attribute it to chance instead of God. There is so much evil around us that we must train ourselves as believers not to fall into the category of people who complain but instead to become those who look out for something good to be thankful for. Of course, the news we hear from the media is also almost entirely bad news, so it is easy to be left feeling very negative. However, we can use that same opportunity to be thankful to God for where we live and pray for those in trouble.

James 3:10 *Out of the same mouth proceed blessing and cursing. My brethren, these things ought not to be so.*

When we cultivate the habit of thankfulness, we disarm the complaining spirit and our lives become more conformed to the Lord Jesus Christ. He always gave thanks to God and did not complain about anything. He addressed the wrong things that happened but did not complain about them.

In Matthew 6:33, God said, *But seek first the Kingdom of God and His righteousness, and all these things shall be added to you.* Obeying this verse will promote thankfulness and reduce complaining. Here, we are commanded to seek God's Kingdom, so our focus should be God's way or order of doing things and not on other things. God is taking care of "all these things" that men seek. If we are seeking after God, our focus will be on His goodness and even when things are not going right, we can still thank God because we know He will fix them as we seek Him.

The Bible urges us to be thankful *in* all things, not *for* all things (of course there are things which are bad or evil) but *in* all things because we know that we have victory in the end. So, we thank God for the victory that we will have in the end. This means looking at our circumstances from the right perspective.

1 Thessalonians 5:18 *In everything give thanks; for this is the will of God in Christ Jesus for you.*

When Jesus was faced with a multitude of hungry people, He gave thanks for the few loaves of bread and fish He had and blessed it.

Mark 6:41 *Taking the five loaves and the two fish and looking up to heaven, He gave thanks and broke the loaves. (NIV)*

When He faced death at the tomb of Lazarus, He gave thanks.

John 11:41 *Then they took away the stone from the place where the dead man was lying. And Jesus lifted up His eyes and said, "Father, I thank You that You have heard Me…"*

Before He drank the wine and ate the bread at the last supper, He gave thanks.

Matthew 26:27 *Then he took a cup, and when he had given thanks, he gave it to them, saying, "Drink from it, all of you."*

In Luke 10:21, Jesus gave thanks to God that He had hidden the secrets of heaven from the wise.

In that hour Jesus rejoiced in the Spirit and said, "I thank You, Father, Lord of heaven and earth, that You have hidden these things from the wise and prudent and revealed them to babes. Even so, Father, for so it seemed good in Your sight.

Jesus did not complain in these challenging situations. He demonstrated the importance of thanksgiving in challenging situations and those situations turned into victories and testimonies of the power of God.

It is easier to give thanks to God when things are going well. Anybody can give thanks to God when everything is going well, but in challenging situations, those who give thanks are those who really trust God. Any normal person complains when faced with challenges but what can inspire us to give thanks to God in challenging situations is when we remember His goodness in the past. Let us learn from Jesus' examples listed above and become more like Him. Our souls do not want to give thanks in adversity. It takes a lot of effort to be grateful in adversity but doing this releases the supernatural power of God.

Complaining can be deadly. This is what prevented the Israelites from entering the promised land. They all died in the wilderness except Joshua and Caleb. May God give us grace to turn the switch from complaining to thanksgiving when faced with challenges.

Thanksgiving dispels fear

Recently, my husband had to undergo a minor surgery. We talked about it and prayed about it before the operation day. On the morning of the surgery, I realized he was still lying in bed even though the time for his appointment was getting close, so I casually asked him the time of the appointment. He replied by asking me what appointment I was talking about. This shocked me because we had talked about it before we slept. Long story short, his mind had gone blank, and he could not remember anything. I tried jolting his memory with a few questions, but he kept saying he could not remember.

At that point, I knew I needed to be strong and pray. I called my oldest child and we agreed in prayer that my husband's memory would be restored. Thankfully, we have trained our children to trust God in adversity, so my son was calm as he confidently prayed with me. After praying, I told my husband to get ready so I could take him to the appointment. (Coincidentally, I had a day off work, so I could drive him there.) All the way to the hospital, we gave thanks and praised God even though my husband kept asking me questions which indicated that his mind was still foggy.

So many thoughts ran through my mind. *What could this mean? Should we cancel the appointment and go and see the family doctor? Would I have to stop working to take care of him?* Many negative thoughts ran through my mind. I knew I had to stop those thoughts and thank God for what He had done already in my husband's health and in the health of our family. I called a couple of prayer partners to pray and kept giving thanks as I waited for him to be taken in for the surgery. The first question he was asked by the nurse was his date of birth, and to the glory of God, he spontaneously remembered correctly.

By the time the surgery was over, he slowly started remembering things. When we got home, I asked the Lord to let him remember one particular thing which was of great importance. Indeed, He did. I thanked God for the grace He gave me to be hopeful instead of being afraid. That hopefulness came from being thankful in the midst of the scary situation. Evidently, fear would have made me make the wrong decision. We would not have gone to get the surgery done and that could have further complicated matters. What took away fear in this situation was thanksgiving.

Thanksgiving opens doors for deliverance

Psalm 50:14–15 *Offer to God thanksgiving, And pay your vows to the Most High. ¹⁵Call upon Me in the day of trouble; I will deliver you, and you shall glorify Me."*

There are various sacrifices we can offer to God. However, thanksgiving should be ranked among the major ones. By recounting and recollecting what God has done and offering thanks to Him, we show that we do not take Him for granted. It is easy to say a simple prayer like "Thank you God for everything," but it does not really mean anything. Once we are careful to bring our specific needs to God, it is also important that we offer thanksgiving prayers to God detailing what He has done. God said when we do that, He will deliver us from trouble so that we can glorify Him. Yes, He will do that because He knows when He delivers us, we will be quick to say thanks to Him and tell others what He has done for us.

The story of Jonah is a unique and interesting one. Jonah thanked God in the belly of the fish and God delivered him.

Jonah 2:9–10 *But I will sacrifice to You with the voice of thanksgiving; I will pay what I have vowed. Salvation is of the Lord." ¹⁰ So the Lord spoke to the fish, and it vomited Jonah onto dry land.*

As important as prayer is for deliverance, there is something even more powerful. It is the power of thanksgiving to God when you are in an impossible situation. This is exactly what Jonah did. I believe Jonah expected to drown when he asked to be thrown into the sea, but God, who caused the storm, also caused the fish to swallow him. Thanksgiving in times of trouble cannot be overemphasized. If we practice what Jonah did, victory is sure because God could do anything to deliver us. He takes delight in delivering us for His glory, but we have to trigger that deliverance with thanksgiving.

Think of times when we have organized Christian programs. We take time to fast and pray—sometimes for days. We pray for the people who will be coming, the weather, the word that will be shared, the venue, the food, protection, direction, our health at that time, flyers to be distributed, souls to be saved, healing, manifestation of the gifts of the spirit, unity, peace and the list can go on and on. But how much time do we spend offering thanksgiving after the program? Do we spend even one hour just giving thanks?

Recently, the Lord asked me to get a few members of the prayer team to start praying and giving thanks after the church service. It was impressed upon my heart that since we always pray before service, it is equally important to give thanks after the service is over. Even if it is not that same day, how many of us spend our next meeting time just giving thanks? We hardly do that. Most of the time, we easily get carried away with the things that did not go right rather than focusing more on what went well because of God's intervention.

It is important to do a review to correct what could have been done better, however, it is even more important to list all the things we prayed for and give thanks to Him for answered prayer. It is also important to thank the people who helped to make the program a success so that they will be encouraged to help again. This may look like an obvious thing to do, but it does not always happen.

Psalm 50:23 *Whoever offers praise glorifies Me;*

Glorifying God means giving Him all the honour and praise for all things and holding Him up to a high place of honour in your heart. We cannot just say, "God, I glorify you." He expects us to thank Him as an outward sign of glorifying Him and not just saying that I glorify you.

Psalm 136:1–26

Oh, give thanks to the Lord, for He is good!
For His mercy endures forever.
² Oh, give thanks to the God of gods!
For His mercy endures forever.
³ Oh, give thanks to the Lord of lords!
For His mercy endures forever:
⁴ To Him who alone does great wonders,
For His mercy endures forever;
⁵ To Him who by wisdom made the heavens,
For His mercy endures forever;
⁶ To Him who laid out the earth above the waters,
For His mercy endures forever;
⁷ To Him who made great lights,
For His mercy endures forever—
⁸ The sun to rule by day,
For His mercy endures forever;
⁹ The moon and stars to rule by night,
For His mercy endures forever.
¹⁰ To Him who struck Egypt in their firstborn,
For His mercy endures forever;
¹¹ And brought out Israel from among them,
For His mercy endures forever;
¹² With a strong hand, and with an outstretched arm,
For His mercy endures forever;
¹³ To Him who divided the Red Sea in two,
For His mercy endures forever;
¹⁴ And made Israel pass through the midst of it,
For His mercy endures forever;
¹⁵ But overthrew Pharaoh and his army in the Red Sea,
For His mercy endures forever;
¹⁶ To Him who led His people through the wilderness,
For His mercy endures forever;
¹⁷ To Him who struck down great kings,
For His mercy endures forever;

*18 And slew famous kings,
For His mercy endures forever—
19 Sihon king of the Amorites,
For His mercy endures forever;
20 And Og king of Bashan,
For His mercy endures forever—
21 And gave their land as a heritage,
For His mercy endures forever;
22 A heritage to Israel His servant,
For His mercy endures forever.
23 Who remembered us in our lowly state,
For His mercy endures forever;
24 And rescued us from our enemies,
For His mercy endures forever;
25 Who gives food to all flesh,
For His mercy endures forever.
26 Oh, give thanks to the God of heaven!
For His mercy endures forever*

Thankfulness is key to strength in times of weakness

Thankfulness will uplift your soul. When a person is weak or physically sick, the situation usually affects their soul. In the same way, when the soul is strong, the body gets strengthened. When we receive a note of appreciation or a word of appreciation, joy comes to our hearts and that joy could provide the needed strength in time of weakness.

3 John 1:2 *Beloved, I pray that you may prosper in all things and be in health, just as your soul prospers.*

For people around us who are struggling, we can remind them of the good things they have done in the past and how grateful we are for their lives. This will certainly lift them up. If they felt like giving up on life, this encouragement might lead them to begin to think differently and realize that their life counts.

Thankfulness allows for the reception of constructive criticism

When you show gratitude to people, those same people are more likely to receive constructive criticism for something they did not do right. People receive criticism based on who it is coming from. If the giver of the criticism is always finding fault, constructive criticism could be rejected. Instead of bringing correction, it could create resentment. Therefore, we should be intentional about appreciating people for the good things they do, especially if we are in a position where we have to provide feedback to the people we oversee.

Thanking God will bring you joy

This is something I have personally experienced. Every time I make up my mind to thank God, my heart is always filled with joy. I smile and tell God, "I was doing this for you, and you chose to bless me with joy." It is such a good feeling that I wouldn't trade for anything. I encourage you to try thanking God when you need joy because you will be able to prove that it works. Remember Nehemiah 8:10, *Do not sorrow, for the joy of the Lord is your strength*. Therefore, thanksgiving should become a lifestyle.

Thankfulness will help you to persevere and not quit

Perseverance is being determined and having an unwavering attitude. It is being steadfast while focusing your attention on pressing on until you achieve your goal. Perseverance is a fruit of the spirit which we need in order to achieve what we aspire for and to fulfill our destinies in life. There could be many opportunities to quit along the journey of life, but it is those who are thankful for what they have already achieved who will be able to persevere to the end.

You may be close to finishing a major project, and then suddenly you hear some news that the project cannot continue due to a new government policy. As a believer, start thanking God for the help He has given you throughout the duration of the project (it may not be easy). Thank Him for wisdom, provision, guidance and every resource available for the project. After that, stand back and watch Him turn things around. I have seen and heard it happen many times, and in the end, what looked like trouble becomes a huge testimony to the glory of God.

A friend got a contract to take care of some international students for a period. The remuneration package was good but just before the contract was to begin, she was informed that the students were unable to come due to reasons beyond their control. Obviously, she had made plans for that money so hearing the contract was going to be cancelled was very disappointing. However, she turned to God with a grateful heart, knowing God could do something about the situation. Shortly after, she heard that only a handful of the students would be allowed to come. She was also advised that her remuneration package would remain intact. This happened because the owner of the place they were going to stay agreed to reduce the rent to its bare minimum—to the point of even running at a loss. This could only be God.

Thankfulness brings hope

When you are thankful, you will have hope for the future. The meaning of hope in the Bible is the confident expectation of what God has promised and its strength is in His faithfulness. Therefore, if we have hope in what God has promised (and there are over 7,000 promises in the Bible), we will be thankful. In the face of despair, gratitude has the power to bring hope.

In times of adversity, thankfulness could remind you that your current situation is not as bad as situations you have already come through. This will give you hope that what you are going through will also pass.

A story was once shared with me in which someone was invited to a church by a friend. After the service, the friend introduced her guest to the pastor in charge and asked him to pray for her because she had been through a series of challenges (bear in mind that the guest did not ask for this). The one who introduced her to the pastor thought she was doing her guest a favour by asking for prayer on her behalf. The pastor started off by asking the guest if she had checked her life to be sure she had not done anything wrong. She responded by saying, "God has been so good to me, what more could I ask for?" As she was sharing the good things God had done in her life, the pastor was so shocked by her reaction that he himself began to worship God.

It is rare to find people who are so grateful even in the face of adversity. Proverbs 4:23 says, *Keep your heart with all diligence, for out of it spring the issues of life.* There was gratitude in the woman's heart and when she was put on the spot, thankfulness is what came out. May we have this attitude of gratitude so that we will only be moved by the goodness of God.

Thankfulness opens doors of opportunity

Growing up, I was taught so often to be thankful that sometimes I did it unconsciously. I must say it has paid off in many ways. When I immigrated to Canada, I got a temporary job, and occasionally the manager would take us out on a business lunch. She did not really have to do that, but she chose to do it to encourage us in our hard work. Each time the lunch was over, I went back to my desk and I wrote her an email saying how much I appreciated her kindness and her taking us out for lunch. I did that just because that was how I was brought up, to be thankful. So, I did just what I knew to do. I did not do it because I wanted to be favoured, but I did it just because I felt it was the right thing to do. One day, the same manager told me she appreciated how polite I was, and apparently, she had been observing me. The long and short of the story is that out of a huge number of people who were on contract at that time, I was among the very few whose contract kept being extended. It pays to be thankful. When you are thankful, people always want to do more for you because just like our Father in heaven, we all want to be appreciated.

Thankful people are humble people

Show me a thankful person and I will show you a humble person. Gratitude comes out of a humble heart. The humble heart is a giving heart; therefore, it identifies the smallest act of kindness shown and focuses on that. On the contrary, proud people are always focused on themselves. In life, there will always be something to complain about, but the humble person picks out the good things that are happening around and shows gratitude for them.

When you realize who you are in Christ, it gives you strength and resilience. This will result in gratitude to God. Otherwise, you could lose purpose and hope in life. Jesus Christ has overcome the world, has made us overcomers in Him and has given us victory. So, we ought to look at things from His perspective.

2 Corinthians 2:14 *Now thanks be to God who always leads us in triumph in Christ, and through us diffuses the fragrance of His knowledge in every place.*

Thank God that you can hear His voice

John 10:27 *My sheep hear My voice, and I know them, and they follow Me.*

What a privilege to hear the voice of the King of Kings and the Lord of Lords. Without hearing His voice, it will be hard to make the right choices that are consistent with God's will for our lives. If He was able to tell Abraham to leave his father's house, then He is still able to give us clear direction. He is the same yesterday, today and forever. Thank God that as children of God we can talk to Him and He talks back to us. We can ask Him questions and He gives us answers. Before the resurrection of Jesus, the prophets and individuals used to have visitations by God and angels to hear from God, but as born-again believers, the Spirit of God lives in us, so we can hear Him speak to us anytime. We do not have to go through any protocol to get to Him. Any moment is okay to talk to Him. Even when we are talking to other people and we need to know how to respond to them, we can be listening to what the Holy Spirit has to say. God does this because He wants a relationship with us, and communication is the best way to maintain a healthy relationship. That is such a blessing!

Unfortunately, some people do not believe that God can speak to us and so have not taken advantage of this great privilege. If you are such a person, I encourage you to ask God to speak to you. Ask Him a question and stay quiet and listen for an answer from within you. Sometimes, it may sound like your own voice because He is speaking through your spirit. This is usually referred to as the inner man. The Lord could either give you a scripture or give an answer that you never expected. Throughout the book of the Acts of the Apostles, God kept speaking to the apostles and even to Gentiles like Cornelius. That privilege is still available to us because we also have the Holy Spirit.

A colleague of mine once asked how I know that it is God speaking back to me. I responded with a question, "Who am I speaking to?" If I am speaking to God in prayer, why should I think it is the devil speaking back to me? One thing you can be sure of (just in case you are confused) is that God will never say anything that is contrary to His word. For example, if you are in dire need of something, God will never suggest to you that you should take something that does not belong to you. That would mean stealing and His word says not to steal. If you are just beginning to hear the voice of God, and you do not know much of the Word of God, it will be a good idea to check with your mentor in Christ when you hear something you are not sure of.

Giving thanks for all people is an instruction

1 Timothy 2:1 *Therefore I exhort first of all that supplications, prayers, intercessions, and giving of thanks be made for all men.*

The apostle Paul urges Christians to give thanks for all people. This is God's expectation when we pray to Him. It is God who answers our prayers. Therefore, it is imperative that we pray according to His will. We should remember that though not all people have chosen to serve God, He still created all people and His desire is that no one person should perish but that everyone will be reconciled back to Him. As we pray according to God's will, we will see the manifestation of His power in the lives of people. There are obviously many reasons to give thanks to God, but we must purposefully do this.

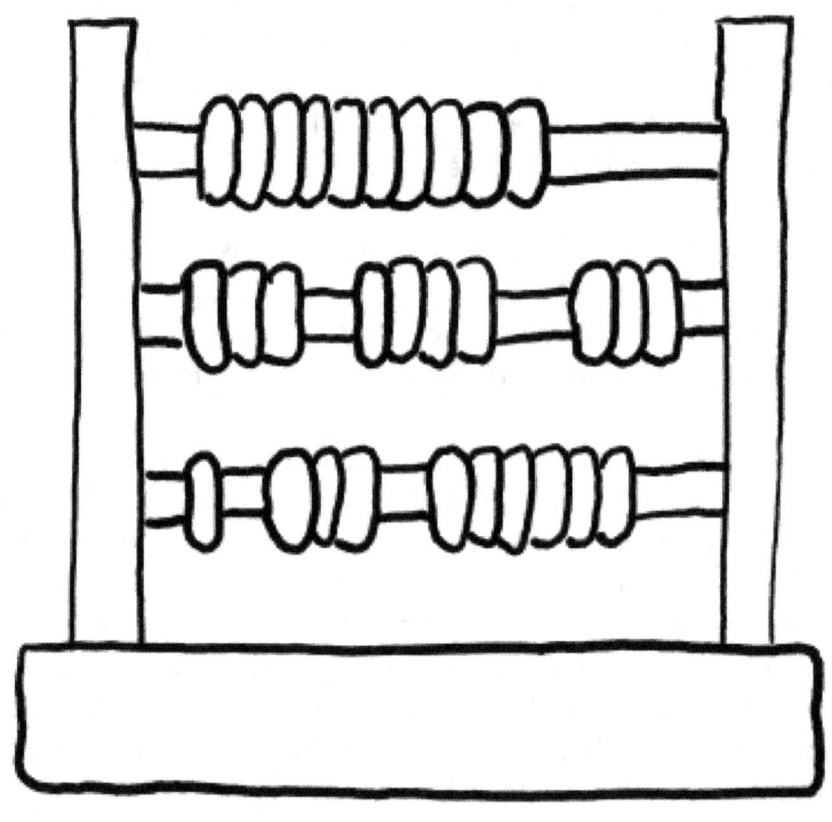

Chapter 2

COUNT YOUR BLESSINGS

The songwriter writes:
"Count your blessings, name them one by one;
Count your blessings, see what God hath done;
Count your blessings, name them one by one,
And it will surprise you what the Lord hath done."

"Count Your Blessings" is a hymn written in 1897 by Johnson Oatman. Giving the reminder to be thankful, "Count Your Blessings" became a very popular hymn with the passage of time. It is important to stop and take time to remember the things God has done. Thank Him. God commanded the Israelites to remember:

Deuteronomy 15:15 *You shall <u>remember</u> that you were a slave in the land of Egypt, and the Lord your God redeemed you; therefore, I command you this thing today.*

It is very easy to forget the many things God has done for us, so it is a good practice to regularly journal the things God does for us. This could be done daily, weekly or monthly. It is also important to keep remembering to give thanks—we need to repeatedly and specifically mention the things He has done. We may have a big breakthrough one day, and a couple of days later when we are faced with a big challenge, we completely forget what happened earlier. We must be intentional about remembering the things God has done.

A forgetful person cannot be thankful. God himself does not forget and that should encourage us not to be forgetful.

Hebrews 6:10 *For God is not unjust to forget your work and labor of love which you have shown toward His name, in that you have ministered to the saints, and do minister.*

Remembrance Day is a memorial day observed in Commonwealth countries. Since the end of the First World War, the world stops to remember the fallen members of their armed forces who died in the line of duty. The nations set aside this day because they acknowledge the value of what the men and women in uniform sacrificed. Yes, they did a great job for our nations, but Jesus has done even greater. How much value do we place on what the Lord Jesus Christ has done for us by giving us eternal life? We should forever be grateful. No matter what comes against us in this world, we can assure ourselves that we have eternal life and we can thank God every day for our salvation.

What are the blessings we are supposed to be counting? Psalm 103 tells us how to be thankful and gives us a list of the blessings we are meant to be thankful for:

¹Bless the Lord, O my soul;
And all that is within me, bless His holy name!

We must command everything in us, all the parts of our body, to bless the Lord. We do this because He created our bodies and sustains them. He causes the blood to flow in our veins and He gives us breath in our lungs. Blessing the Lord is a command and not a suggestion.

² Bless the Lord, O my soul,
And forget not all His benefits:

It is our responsibility to remember the things God has done for us and be grateful for them. To me, this is as important as remembering to pay our bills. Whatever we consider important in life, we do everything to remember them. For some individuals, it is exercising. For others, it is remembering certain birthdays or special events and honouring them. We go to any extent to make sure we do not forget. In the same way, we can add a quick reminder on our calendars to make note of the things God has done for us and remember to give thanks.

[3] *Who forgives all your iniquities,*
Who heals all your diseases,

If we have ever forgiven someone, which I hope we all have, we will know that it is a sacrifice. This is because our flesh wants to pay the person back for what they did to us. To truly forgive, we have to deny our flesh of what it wants in order to obey God. It is not easy to forgive until we have experienced the forgiveness of God. The fact that God forgives us of every iniquity is huge. This includes lies, all immoral acts and even murder, yes, even murder. God forgives us when we repent and confess our sins and He remembers them no more.

Hebrews 8:12 *For I will be merciful to their unrighteousness, and their sin and their lawless deeds I will remember no more.*

Indeed, God will forgive any kind of sin. Serial killing, adultery and fornication, hatred, cheating, sexual perversion, rebellion, witchcraft, idolatry—He forgives them all. Jesus forgave the murderer on the cross next to Him. This was a demonstration of God's willingness to forgive no matter what you have done. In the book of Acts, we see that He forgave Saul who helped to murder believers. We must be thankful for God's forgiveness. Some other gods could strike their followers with death when they break a rule, but God's loving-kindness is endless. He is slow to anger and plenteous in mercy. Thank you, Lord. Take stock of how many times we wrong God in a day through our evil thoughts, careless actions and our sheer disobedience. Therefore, we must be thankful each day that He forgives us.

I believe that God in His kindness not only heals us of the diseases that doctors have diagnosed us of, but that He also heals us of sicknesses in our bodies that we do not even know we have. Medicine only takes care of symptoms, but as the psalmist writes, it is God who has the capability to heal all our diseases since He created our bodies. God is gracious enough to heal even those who do not believe in Him. He makes the sun rise on both the evil and the good.

Matthew 5:45 *that you may be sons of your Father in heaven; for He makes His sun rise on the evil and on the good and sends rain on the just and on the unjust.*

We should thank Him daily for this reason. Even if we do not feel well, we can be thankful for the healing we have enjoyed in the past. Everyone has experienced one form of healing or another because everyone experiences at least some symptoms of sickness due to the fallen nature of man. Continuing to live is a sign that God has been healing us. He is Jehovah Rapha, the Lord who heals.

[4]*Who redeems your life from destruction,*
Who crowns you with lovingkindness and tender mercies

The word "redeem" here means to buy back. Jesus paid the ransom for our souls. This is love. He paid the price we had to pay for our sins. He delivered us from the pit of hell. He fights our spiritual battles when we engage in prayer, since we are not fighting against flesh and blood but against principalities, powers and wicked spirits. He delivers us from many calamities. He loves us with an unfailing love and He never gives up on us. "He crowns us with loving kindness" means He heaps on us or loads us with blessings. For these reasons, we must give Him thanks.

*⁵Who satisfies your mouth with good things,
So that your youth is renewed like the eagle's.*

Good and nutritious food comes from the Lord. He is the source of our provision. He gives bread to the eater to renew his strength. The eagle is the most powerful bird with its focus and great vision. We can be thankful that God provides food for us and makes us as strong and powerful as eagles. I have heard of a woman who has been declaring this verse for years in her adult life. She is now over eighty years old and is as strong as when she was in her youth. She drives for long hours to visit family and visits the elderly with warm food (even though she is elderly herself). Isn't that amazing?

*⁶The Lord executes righteousness
And justice for all who are oppressed*

We are made righteous through Christ Jesus so that we can be in right standing with God. We must thank God for giving us justice from our oppressor, the enemy of our souls. If God does not acquit and discharge us, the enemy will not let us go free. When we repent before God, He forgives us and acquits us of any charges the enemy brings against us. Praise the Lord.

*⁷He made known His ways to Moses,
His acts to the children of Israel*

We can be thankful to God for revealing Himself to us through the rhema of His word just as He did to Moses. He does this through the power of the Holy Spirit. When we read the Word of God, we get revelation through the Holy Spirit so that we can apply that scripture to our lives to give us direction on how to fulfill our destinies in life.

⁸The Lord is merciful and gracious,
Slow to anger, and abounding in mercy

Indeed, God is merciful and gracious. Consider how many times we sin against Him and repent for the same sins. Sometimes, we even repent daily for the same sins, yet He is merciful to forgive us because He does not break His covenant. He says that if we confess our sins, He is faithful and just to forgive us and to cleanse us from all unrighteousness (1 John 1:9). He is slow to get angry, and that is why He has not destroyed the world. He wants to give all men the opportunity to repent and come to the saving knowledge of Jesus Christ. For this we should be thankful.

⁹He will not always strive with us,
Nor will He keep His anger forever

Even though God was angry with mankind when we sold our birthright to the devil, He did not keep His anger forever. He sent Jesus Christ, His only son, to die for our sin—which we could not pay for—so that we could be reconciled back to Him. Some people think He is an angry God who is waiting to punish us, but that is not true. He is a merciful God who continually has to deal with rebellious people. He does not remain angry so that He can save us.

¹⁰He has not dealt with us according to our sins,
Nor punished us according to our iniquities

The Bible tells us that there are consequences for sin, and the punishment for sin is death (Romans 6:23). Instead of putting that punishment on us, He has given us salvation through Jesus Christ. If we accept Jesus as the substitute for our sins, our punishment is put on Him. That is awesome. When we take some time to reflect on the details, it should move us to gratitude. Thank God He does not punish us according to the magnitude of our sins and iniquities. If He did that, I am sure we would all be destroyed.

As I wrote this chapter, the Lord reminded me of something that I did wrong over twenty-five years ago. At that time, I didn't think it was a big deal. I never repented of it even though it crossed my mind a few times. I just swept it under the rug. However, during my devotion this morning, He brought it up again, and I knew I had to repent of it. I just began to thank God after repenting for being so merciful to me in my carelessness.

[11]*For as the heavens are high above the earth,*
So great is His mercy toward those who fear Him.

In Psalm 103:11, the Lord continues to describe to us the extent of His mercies toward those who fear Him. His mercies are unending. Who can measure the distance between the heavens and the earth? Scientists have found no end to the universe. This indicates how much mercy He has toward His children. Thank God for His mercies.

[12]*As far as the east is from the west,*
So far has He removed our transgressions from us.

Jesus' love has removed our sins from us. He died on the cross to take away our sins for good. This verse continues to emphasize His forgiveness. It also reiterates the fact that there is no limit to His mercies and love. It confirms that He no longer remembers our sins once we are forgiven. Praise the Lord.

[13]*As a father pities his children,*
So, the Lord pities those who fear Him

The Lord empathizes with the pain and sorrow that those who fear Him go through. He shares in that pain because He truly understands and for that we thank Him. Jesus went through the same pains we go through having suffered under the wickedness of the Jewish leaders. The Bible says Jesus learnt obedience through suffering, so He truly understands our afflictions (Hebrews 5:8).

14 For He knows our frame.
He remembers that we are dust.

Because He made us, the Lord understands that we are partly flesh and blood and does not forget our human frailties. We like to relate with people who understand us, and the Lord understands us just as we are and for that reason, we must thank Him.

The remaining part of Psalm 103 states:

15 As for man, his days are like grass.
As a flower of the field, so he flourishes.
16 For the wind passes over it, and it is gone,
And its place remembers it no more.
17 But the mercy of the Lord is from everlasting to everlasting
On those who fear Him,
And His righteousness to children's children,
18 To such as keep His covenant,
And to those who remember His commandments to do them

The mercies of God are mentioned once again. It appears to me that God stresses on the availability of His mercies to emphasize the importance of it. Without the mercies of God, no man will be deserving of any good thing. Even our good deeds without Him are like dirty rags.

Isaiah 64:6 *But we are all like an unclean thing, And all our righteousness are like filthy rags; We all fade as a leaf, And our iniquities, like the wind, have taken us away.*

God needs to show us mercy so that we can receive His goodness. How can we stand before a Holy God without feeling condemned—a God who is light, a God in whom there is no darkness at all? Our perfection can only come from the cleansing blood of Jesus. We will always need God's mercies and thank God they will always be available for us. We should remember that we do not deserve anything. Everything we have is by His grace. If we begin to think we have earned what we have received, we will not be truly grateful because we will think it was our doing. However, if we know that every little thing is by His grace, then we will appreciate everything and be thankful to God. It is very easy to get into the mode of thinking we have worked hard as Christians for God, so we deserve something. It is all His grace. Understanding this will keep us humble and always grateful.

Even though God's mercies are from everlasting to everlasting, He renews them every morning. They are refreshed every morning. Though He may have shown great mercy to us today, that will not limit the mercy He will show us tomorrow or in the days and months following. Thank God for His mercies!

Lamentations 3:22–23 *Through the Lord's mercies we are not consumed, Because His compassions fail not.* [23]*They are new every morning; Great is Your faithfulness*

God wants us to remember the things He has done for us so that we can be grateful. It is important to have a symbol of remembrance because sometimes we easily forget where we came from. When God dried up the Jordan river for Joshua and the Israelites to walk through, He instructed him to have twelve men, one from each tribe, to get a stone from the river to serve as a memorial for their children so that they would remember what He, the Lord, did for them.

Joshua 4:4–7 So Joshua called together the twelve men he had appointed from the Israelites, one from each tribe, ⁵ and said to them, "Go over before the ark of the Lord your God into the middle of the Jordan. Each of you is to take up a stone on his shoulder, according to the number of the tribes of the Israelites, ⁶ to serve as a sign among you. In the future, when your children ask you, 'What do these stones mean?' ⁷ tell them that the flow of the Jordan was cut off before the ark of the covenant of the Lord.

God expected the Israelites to remember His goodness from generation to generation because it is very easy for us to forget the great things God has done, especially when things get tough. The lesson here is that God wants us to tell about His goodness from generation to generation so that they will have reason to thank him.

Sometimes, even the heathen remembers what the Almighty God does for His people and they tremble at the thought of that. Below is what Rahab the harlot told the two spies sent to Jericho by Joshua.

Joshua 2:9–11 And she said unto the men, I know that the Lord hath given you the land, and that your terror is fallen upon us, and that all the inhabitants of the land faint because of you.¹⁰ For we have heard how the Lord dried up the water of the Red sea for you, when ye came out of Egypt; and what ye did unto the two kings of the Amorites, that were on the other side Jordan, Sihon and Og, whom ye utterly destroyed.
¹¹ And as soon as we had heard these things, our hearts did melt, neither did there remain any more courage in any man, because of you: for the Lord your God, he is God in heaven above, and in earth beneath

When people travel on vacations, they try to buy souvenirs to bring back memories of the location they travelled to. God wants us to have memories of the things He does for us so that we will be thankful.

One time, I was in a difficult place financially, and I really felt like withdrawing from a financial commitment I had made. I must say that by the grace of God I am not a quitter, however, I had really been pushed to the wall in this situation, and I was really moved to quit. Around that same time, my husband and I were invited to an event for a charity that we supported. While there, they had people draw for prizes, and I won the first prize. For the record, I hardly win things like that, so I knew it was God. Driving back home, the Lord began to speak to me about the prize I won (a souvenir) and how it should be a sign that He will take care of that situation I wanted to quit from. That prize still sits on my mantlepiece and anytime I look at it, it tells me not to quit. I must say God was faithful in providing for me so that I could carry out that financial commitment which required me to give monthly.

Some people have scars on their bodies, and those scars are reminders of how God healed them. When I was much younger, I had a boil on my thigh—a very big and painful one. God healed me, but the scar is still there, and I cannot forget what it stands for. If you have any scar like that on your body, always remember God as your healer and thank Him. Those scars can also be a source of encouragement when you have a physical challenge that God who healed you will do it again. Praise the Lord! Remember, this is part of counting our blessings.

Counting your blessings in times of crisis

When the Ammonites and Moabites declared war on Israel in 2 Chronicles 20, Jehoshaphat did something noteworthy as he went to inquire of the Lord. He worshipped God and counted the blessings God had bestowed in Israel:

2 Chronicles 20:7–9 Are You not our God, who drove out the inhabitants of this land before Your people Israel, and gave it to the descendants of Abraham Your friend forever? ⁸ And they dwell in it and have built You a sanctuary in it for Your name, saying, ⁹ 'If disaster comes upon us—sword, judgment, pestilence, or famine—we will stand before this temple and in Your presence (for Your name is in this temple), and cry out to You in our affliction, and You will hear and save.'

Jehoshaphat recounted what God had done and knew that He would do it again. We see God did it again as the story unfolds. The Lord gave a battle strategy, and the Israelites had victory again which added to their lists of blessings.

Counting your blessings in times of crisis gives you confidence for the situation you are facing. Sometimes, as you do that, you realize that what God has already brought you through was even greater than the situation you are currently facing. This gives you rest in your spirit, which is what you need in your current situation. Jehoshaphat needed a word from God, but first he glorified Him for what He had already done. It was after this that God gave him the strategy for the current situation. By counting your blessings in times of crisis, you are letting the enemy know that you are certain God will deliver you.

When David faced Goliath, his confidence came from recounting what God had already done for him.

1 Samuel 17:31–37 Now when the words which David spoke were heard, they reported them to Saul; and he sent for him. ³² Then David said to Saul, "Let no man's heart fail because of him; your servant will go and fight with this Philistine."

33 And Saul said to David, "You are not able to go against this Philistine to fight with him; for you are a youth, and he a man of war from his youth."
34 But David said to Saul, "Your servant used to keep his father's sheep, and when a lion or a bear came and took a lamb out of the flock, 35 I went out after it and struck it, and delivered the lamb from its mouth; and when it arose against me, I caught it by its beard, and struck and killed it. 36 Your servant has killed both lion and bear; and this uncircumcised Philistine will be like one of them, seeing he has defied the armies of the living God." 37 Moreover David said, "The Lord, who delivered me from the paw of the lion and from the paw of the bear, He will deliver me from the hand of this Philistine."

It was important for David to recollect what God had already done so that he could put the situation into the right perspective. Here was a very young man facing a fully armed giant. Goliath's appearance alone was enough to intimidate a fully armed soldier. In addition to his intimidating appearance, he was issuing threats against God's people. By glorifying God for what He had already done, David assured himself that God would do it again as Goliath was no match for his God.

When we glorify God amid a challenge, it shows that we trust God and trust that we will never be put to shame. I believe when David recollected what God had done, he received inspiration for what he was about to deal with. Sometimes, we face situations which are daunting and look impossible. We must first remember the God and Father to whom we belong. The best way to remember His greatness and power is to take the Word of God and begin to read some of the Psalms which describe who He is. Of course, David wrote most of the book of Psalms, so he knew how to declare the greatness of God.

It is in our interest to count our blessings in a time of crisis because it keeps our focus off the crisis and instead on Jesus. The more you count your blessings, the more your faith in

God increases. It is very easy in times of crisis to focus on the problem instead of focusing on the God who can bring you out of that problem. Whatever you focus on becomes bigger; that is why the apostle Paul urges us to keep our eyes on Jesus who is the author and finisher of our faith. When we keep our eyes on Jesus and what He has already done, He becomes bigger than the situation we find ourselves in. One sure way of making Him our focus is recounting the things he has done in our lives.

Revelations 12:11 *And they overcame him by the blood of the Lamb and by the word of their testimony, and they did not love their lives to the death.*

Counting our blessings is one of the invincible weapons in the believer's arsenal to overcome the enemy. Testimonies are simply recounting what God has done for you and letting others know. Whenever there is an opportunity to testify, we must take advantage of it because by doing this we defeat the devil. Some people are shy to share testimonies, but testimonies glorify God and encourage others to also trust God. I personally thrive on testimonies. To me, testimonies are proof that the Bible is true, and that God is as true and real as the Bible says He is.

Hebrews 13:8 *Jesus Christ is the same yesterday, today, and forever*

As much as testimonies glorify God, they are also a powerful channel for reaching the lost. Testimonies are as powerful as the preaching of the Word of God. The Full Gospel Business Men's Fellowship International reaches out to the lost souls through testimonies. Many people have come to faith in the Lord Jesus Christ as their personal Saviour through the personal testimonies that are shared by members of the fellowship. Listening to these testimonies generates faith in the unbelievers and releases God's transformative power upon their lives. For those who already know the Lord and are going through challenging times, testimonies provide inspiration that God will do what He has promised to do, regardless of how long it takes or how difficult the situation might be.

Interestingly, the Bible is full of testimonies of what God did in the lives of the men and women of old. Today, these testimonies provide strength, hope and encouragement as we walk the Christian path. The power of testimonies becomes even more apparent when you base your prayer on a testimony of someone in the Bible, and then see the evidence of that in your own life. The testimony of any of the biblical characters is evidence to us that God is still in the business of transforming lives today.

My own life is a testimony to the power of God. Let me share a recent experience that attests to the faithfulness of God. God's favour can change or make a way where there is no way so that you get what you need. In this particular case, the life of Queen Esther served as the specific testimony the Lord used to work in my life.

I saw that after spending time waiting on the Lord in prayer and fasting, Queen Esther approached the King, submitted her request and got what she needed. God intervened. Even the protocols of approaching the King's throne were set aside for her sake. She walked into the King's presence even when it was not the king who commanded her to be brought into his presence.

In the same way, I needed a travel document processed for someone. However, there was one mandatory requirement that was missing. Due to time constraints, it was not possible to wait until the requirement was brought in. After praying and inquiring of the Lord whether the person was to travel, I felt a prompting to take the available paperwork and trust Him that the travel document would be issued. Ordinarily, the application should have been rejected until the missing requirement was brought in. That is the usual protocol. I and the one I was applying for was going to be embarrassed if the application was rejected. Yet, I chose to trust the Lord and put His word to the test. Indeed, He proved Himself faithful. The travel document was processed, and no mention was made of the missing requirement.

This really blessed my heart and encouraged me in my walk with God. Sometimes, He will prevent you from getting into the fiery furnace, and other times, He will be with you in the fire and bring you out without the smell of smoke. He is indeed a good God. As you read my testimony, I trust that faith will arise in you and you will dare to use your faith to do something unusual so that you can have a reason to be thankful to God and be a blessing to others.

There is another thing God did for me when I was in high school which I still remember vividly. A new school term was beginning, and I really wanted new shoes. This wasn't because I didn't have shoes, but I just wanted something new to show off at school. I prayed and asked God for new shoes because I knew my grandma, who I was living with, would not get me new shoes just because I wanted them. I was attending boarding school and I was going to be dropped off at school around 5 p.m. that day. At 2 p.m., before leaving, we had a visitor arrive at our house. He had just arrived from the States where my Dad lived and brought with him a package for me. In the package from my Dad was a pair of shoes. You can imagine my excitement. I still remember it until today. I was not expecting anything from my Dad at that time and the timing could not have been better. I was so thankful to God and that encouraged my trust in Him and I believe He sat in heaven smiling that He had made me so happy.

Testimonies inevitably revel to us how great God is. Some people unfortunately believe that sickness and poverty glorify God, but it is the other way around—it is the healings and the supernatural provision of God which bring glory to God. It is only God who can truly heal a terminally ill person. Unbelievers will believe in Jesus when they see these miracles and that is why we need to testify. Believers believe what they have not seen, but unbelievers believe by what they see. Make it a habit to count your blessings. It is a choice you have to make daily. Live as an overcomer by counting your blessings. The more you count your blessings, the more blessings will be added to you.

God grieved over Israel for not remembering what he had done for them. That is what happens when we soon forget the things God does for us. He expects us to remember them so that we are assured of His faithfulness.

Micah 6:3–5 *"O My people, what have I done to you? And how have I wearied you? Testify against Me. ⁴For I brought you up from the land of Egypt, I redeemed you from the house of bondage; And I sent before you Moses, Aaron, and Miriam. ⁵O My people, remember now What Balak king of Moab counseled, And what Balaam the son of Beor answered him, From Acacia Grove to Gilgal, That you may know the righteousness of the Lord."*

A study was conducted by the University of California that tested the act of counting your blessings versus counting your burdens. The effect of a grateful outlook on psychological and physical well-being was examined. Participants were randomly assigned to one of three experiments to compare the effects of keeping records of difficulties, things they were grateful for, or neutral life events. They also kept records of their moods and how they coped with the situations. The outcome showed that those who focused on things they were grateful for may have had emotional and interpersonal benefits. It also had a positive effect on their physical and psychological health (Emmons and McCullough).

Thank God for not allowing you to have what you wanted but were not ready for

There are most likely disappointments in our lives that we are grateful to God for today. There are things we have asked God for that He did not allow us to have. We were disappointed and possibly heartbroken, only to find out later that it was God's gracious hand delivering us out of trouble we could not have handled. You may have desperately wanted to marry someone and along the way you had to breakup, only to find out that he was already in another relationship. This person would certainly be the wrong candidate if God had not allowed the breakup. It could be a job you didn't get or a business contract that didn't go through. In protecting us, He will sometimes not allow some things to work out so that His will can be done in our lives because He loves us so much.

I was meditating on Jacob's marriage to Leah and Rachel. Jacob did not love Leah and in his heart, it was Rachel he wanted. However, in God's plan for Israel, twelve tribes were going to come out of Jacob who became Israel. Rachael only gave birth to two of those tribes. God knew that Leah was part of that plan, so even though Laban deceived him by giving Leah to him instead of Rachel, it all worked together for the good in the end.

I just began to think of how our selfish desires can sometimes get in the way of what God wants to do with our lives. I wonder how many opportunities we may have missed because we wanted our own way in a situation. Thank God Jacob did not abandon Leah though he didn't love her. For the love of Rachel, he accepted Leah and worked seven more years after he married Rachel. As a result of that, we have the twelve tribes of Israel. What looked like a punishment became a blessing to Jacob and his descendants. As we trust God for answers to our prayers, may we be thankful also that He did not allow certain things to go our way so that His perfect will could be done in our lives.

Think about this: what if you woke up every day excited about the plans God had for you and went to bed recollecting and writing down all the good things that happened? Doing this could shift the focus of what needs to be done that day to looking forward to the testimonies that will come forth.

Chapter 3

SMILE

Smiling is an outward expression of an inner gratitude. In other words, when we smile, we demonstrate that we are thankful about something. We smile when we are pleased about something or when we are positive that something good is going to happen. What if we choose to smile by faith so that although there is nothing happening around us that makes us smile, we create the environment for something good to happen? When we hear good news, we smile. When someone gives us a compliment, we smile. When we have a good dream, we smile. When we get a raise at work or a promotion, we smile. When we get an unexpected discount, we smile.

A smile relaxes our muscles and tells our body that all is well. Research confirms that when a smile flashes across your face, dopamine, endorphins and serotonin are all released into your bloodstream, making not only your body relax, but it also works to lower your heart rate and blood pressure.

<u>Benefits of smiling</u>

According to NeuroNation, smiling helps toward fighting stress. A smile releases dopamine, endorphins and serotonin which make the body relax and lowers blood pressure. Additionally, endorphins are natural pain killers which obviously have no side effects. Smiling is infectious because the part of your brain that is responsible for your facial expression of smiling when happy or mimicking another person's smile is located in the cingulate cortex, an unconscious automatic response area. This confirms that when you smile at someone, they naturally tend to smile back. (NeuroNation)

When we choose to smile during times of adversity, it is because we remember the good things that happened in the past, and we know and believe that it will happen again. We can smile in adversity because we know the greater one lives in us. We can smile in adversity when we know what the Word of God says about the situation. Smiling attracts and can bring good things our way. Smiling is to say that all is well, so we do not have to wait for all to be well before we choose to smile. We can create the environment for all to be well.

When you leave your house with a smile and you keep that smile, most of the people you meet will smile back at you. They will smile not because they know you or they share anything in common with you, but it is because smiling means something good is happening and everyone wants to associate with what is good. You can easily make a friend just because you were smiling. Have you been in a situation when you just heard something that devastated you, and as you walked along the street, someone smiles at you? At that moment, a ray of light is thrown at you and all the darkness around you seems to disappear. You forget for a while all the bad news you heard and smile back. As you smile, you begin to receive energy.

Smiling at someone you do not know could mean a sign of respect for that person. Someone may be going through rejection and that smile could make him feel accepted. That smile could remain with that person for a long time. Imagine walking into an auditorium where you cannot find the one who invited you, and you begin to look out for someone with a smile to ask for directions or assistance.

Couples have met each other through a smile. Smiling at an in-person interview could be what stands out between you and another person who gets the same mark as you. Since the smile causes attraction, you could stand a better chance of getting the job.

Even your worst enemy cannot resist a sincere smile. Smiling as an expression of kindness, even when people know they do not deserve that smile, can cripple their wicked intentions.

Smiling while you are chatting with someone on the phone or skype could be felt by the person or persons you are communicating with. Presenters are encouraged to smile at their audience though they may not see them. The conversation feels more relaxed and the voice is stronger and more positive while in that conversation.

Job 9:27 *If I say, 'I will forget my complaint, I will put off my sad face and wear a smile,'*

As Job said, you cannot be smiling and thinking about problems at the same time. Even in the midst of his adversities, he could choose to smile if he wanted to, but he could not forget his problems. By our strength, it is almost impossible to forget our problems, but with the help of God, we can cast every care on Him and begin to smile again. It will make our spirit lighter and as we take that step of faith, God will bring the solution.

Some people naturally have smiling faces. That is such a blessing. It is so welcoming. Those people are attractive not because of their looks but because of their smile which in turn becomes part of their looks. The good thing is that we can all practice wearing a smiling face until it becomes a part of us. Some people also always choose to wear a frown and it is almost impossible to get them to smile. In fact, they may even get very uncomfortable with people who smile all the time. It is all a choice. It may not be easy if you do not have the Holy Spirit living in you. But if you do, you can make the decision to smile and He will help you maintain the smile.

Does it take effort to smile when there is nothing exciting to smile about? Yes it does, but with practice, it will take less effort.

It becomes a habit over time, and eventually it becomes your second nature. You will wake up smiling and go to bed smiling. Even when you cry, you will end up smiling. Even when you get angry, you will end up smiling once it becomes a habit.

The apostle Paul says:

Philippians 4:4 *Rejoice in the Lord always. Again, I will say, rejoice!*

He wrote this in prison. There was nothing to be excited about in a smelly dungeon, but the power of God through the Holy Spirit inside of him could make him smile. Paul put emphasis on rejoicing, repeating it in the same verse. Obviously, it is an instruction which needs to be carried out. The good part of this instruction to rejoice is that it is a choice. You can choose to rejoice just as you choose to sleep or eat. In other words, I don't have to wait for anything special to happen in my life to rejoice. If Paul had waited for everything to be perfect in his life before rejoicing, we may never have read his letters which is about two-thirds of the New Testament.

You cannot rejoice without smiling. Smiling shows what is going on inside you. Smiling reflects joy inside you and joy equals strength.

Nehemiah 8:10 *the joy of the Lord is your strength."*

Therefore, it is important that we bring out that joy inside us which is a fruit of the spirit. This joy which will make us smile is based on our relationship with Jesus and not on outward occurrences. Though outward occurrences can make us joyful and make us smile, they are very short lived. It is interesting how you can hear some good news (e.g. you got a job you really wanted) and for the first week, you are so excited. Give it one week or two and you could go back into depression because that joy is not driven from within, so it does not last. The joy which is derived from the Spirit of God coming from within you, can be sustained so long as you maintain your relationship with the Holy Spirit—praying and studying the Word of God.

Smiling is also important because it is the outward sign of a grateful heart or a thankful heart. It stems out of a heart that is meditating on good things. Paul continues in this same chapter of Philippians to teach us what thoughts can make us rejoice.

Philippians 4:8 *Finally, brethren, whatever things are true, whatever things are noble, whatever things are just, whatever things are pure, whatever things are lovely, whatever things are of good report, if there is any virtue and if there is anything praiseworthy—meditate on these things.*

Thinking on the things mentioned above will make you smile. We choose either to smile, to frown, or to have a blank facial expression. The latter two will not profit us anything, but maintaining a smile could have a positive impact on us and on others.

When my youngest daughter was about three years old, she came to tell us after a Sunday school class that whenever she got to the class, everyone would start smiling and the reason was she had an infectious smile. She was encouraged to continue smiling because she knew it was affecting others positively. She left a lasting impression on people's mind because of her smile. People remembered her because of her smile.

The world is going through so much turmoil and they do not know how to handle it. As believers, we go through the same struggles, but the Spirit of God in us gives us the ability to smile through the tough times. This does not make sense to the world. When we choose to smile, we focus on the goodness of God and are thankful for what He has done and what He is about to do and not what we are going through.

Romans 8:19 *For the earnest expectation of the creation eagerly waits for the revealing of the sons of God.*

    The whole earth is waiting for the manifestation of the sons of God; we have the answers through Christ Jesus because we have the Word of God.

    Smiling as a child of God could also be a sign of gratitude to God. Just thinking about the goodness of God can make you smile and while you smile, someone could ask why, and you could share how thankful you are to God.

    Some people do not smile because they are not satisfied with the way they look. That is ungratefulness to God who created you in his own image. I have heard people make fun of others because of their looks, sometimes even right in front of them, but that is an insult to God because He created mankind in His own image. Such comments make some people feel so bad about themselves that they will not smile. However, if you are a Christian who believes that the Word of God is true, then you will believe what the Bible says.

Psalm 139:14 *I will praise You, for I am fearfully and wonderfully made; Marvelous are Your works, And that my soul knows very well.*

    Does your soul know that you are fearfully and wonderfully made by God or are you believing what others are saying about you? Be your own cheerleader. Love yourself because you appreciate how God created you and others will love you. Sometimes, we wait for affirmation from people to give us confidence to smile, but we should let the Word of God be enough affirmation for us. It is not wrong to get affirmation from others, but it is better to believe what God has said about you, so whether you get affirmation from others or not, your heart is established on what God has said concerning you and your confidence remains intact.

Genesis 1:27 So God created man in His own image; in the image of God He created him; male and female He created them.

Dare to believe that the above scripture is true. If you believe you were created in the image of God, then you ought to like the way you look. My daughter made another comment when she was about the same age—one day, she looked in the mirror after I had dressed her up and she said, "I love myself." We were all surprised at that profound statement, but the fact is, if you do not love yourself, why do you think someone should love you?

Some people have had multiple surgeries to change their looks because of a comment someone made which caused them to feel that they do not belong. Some always want to resemble people who the world thinks are the standard of what good-looking people should look like. Unfortunately, no matter how much man tries to fix the outside looks, if the inside of that person is empty, or not filled with Jesus Christ to be precise, it will be meaningless. It may bring some instant gratification, but when the enemy begins to bring negative thoughts to you, then the realization comes that nothing can satisfy the void inside of you but Christ. It is not the way you look, or the way people see you that matters, but what God says about you.

The Bible says a merry heart is like medicine. It is medicine for the soul which can benefit the body. A merry heart cannot hide. No one can be merry and frown. A merry heart shows through a smile. If a merry heart is like medicine, then why don't we make the effort to have a merry heart and smile? If we visit a doctor and he gives us a prescription which can heal a disease, we gladly go and buy it or look for money to get the prescription. I believe we can all use this free prescription—a merry heart. If we choose not to use it, the opposite applies. A heart that is not merry will end up becoming broken and this can have a negative impact on the body. So, we cannot just get away with not having a merry heart. It has negative consequences. May we make every effort to choose to be merry and smile.

Proverbs 17:22 *A merry heart does good, like medicine, But a broken spirit dries the bones.*

Let's begin to practice smiling regularly. We can even make ourselves accountable to each other such that the other party can ensure we are smiling all the time. I do this with my sister who lives in another country. On a regular basis, she will send me a text—SMILE—and regardless of what's going on in my day, I stop and smile. I do the same with her and we both find it to be a blessing. We do ourselves a favor when we smile, and we can be thankful that we can wear a smile.

Chapter 4

APPRECIATE NATURE

Appreciating nature means appreciating God's mighty hand in the created order. More than the esteem or fame that an artist experiences when his or her work is appreciated, the appreciation of nature is a personal declaration that God is the Creator of the heavens and the earth. Genesis Chapter 1 fully outlines all the things He created, and He Himself acknowledged them as good. God created everything that man would need to live on earth before He even created man and that is why we should appreciate nature. Nature is beautiful and refreshing to the soul. Man is God's masterpiece and the seal of all his creation.

Genesis 1:4–29 *⁴And God saw the light, that it was good; and God divided the light from the darkness. ⁵God called the light Day, and the darkness He called Night. So the evening and the morning were the first day.*

⁶Then God said, "Let there be a firmament in the midst of the waters, and let it divide the waters from the waters." ⁷Thus God made the firmament, and divided the waters which were under the firmament from the waters which were above the firmament; and it was so. ⁸And God called the firmament Heaven. So the evening and the morning were the second day.

⁹Then God said, "Let the waters under the heavens be gathered together into one place, and let the dry land appear"; and it was so. ¹⁰And God called the dry land Earth, and the gathering together of the waters He called Seas. And God saw that it was good.

[11]Then God said, "Let the earth bring forth grass, the herb that yields seed, and the fruit tree that yields fruit according to its kind, whose seed is in itself, on the earth"; and it was so. [12]And the earth brought forth grass, the herb that yields seed according to its kind, and the tree that yields fruit, whose seed is in itself according to its kind. And God saw that it was good. [13]So the evening and the morning were the third day.

[14]Then God said, "Let there be lights in the firmament of the heavens to divide the day from the night; and let them be for signs and seasons, and for days and years; [15]and let them be for lights in the firmament of the heavens to give light on the earth"; and it was so.[16]Then God made two great lights: the greater light to rule the day, and the lesser light to rule the night. He made the stars also. [17]God set them in the firmament of the heavens to give light on the earth, [18]and to rule over the day and over the night, and to divide the light from the darkness. And God saw that it was good. [19]So the evening and the morning were the fourth day.

[20]Then God said, "Let the waters abound with an abundance of living creatures, and let birds fly above the earth across the face of the firmament of the heavens." [21]So God created great sea creatures and every living thing that moves, with which the waters abounded, according to their kind, and every winged bird according to its kind. And God saw that it was good. [22]And God blessed them, saying, "Be fruitful and multiply, and fill the waters in the seas, and let birds multiply on the earth." [23]So the evening and the morning were the fifth day.

[24]Then God said, "Let the earth bring forth the living creature according to its kind: cattle and creeping thing and beast of the earth, each according to its kind"; and it was so. [25]And God made the beast of the earth according to its kind, cattle

according to its kind, and everything that creeps on the earth according to its kind. And God saw that it was good.

²⁶Then God said, "Let Us make man in Our image, according to Our likeness; let them have dominion over the fish of the sea, over the birds of the air, and over the cattle, over all the earth and over every creeping thing that creeps on the earth." ²⁷So God created man in His own image; in the image of God He created him; male and female He created them. ²⁸Then God blessed them, and God said to them, "Be fruitful and multiply; fill the earth and subdue it; have dominion over the fish of the sea, over the birds of the air, and over every living thing that moves on the earth."

²⁹And God said, "See, I have given you every herb that yields seed which is on the face of all the earth, and every tree whose fruit yields seed; to you it shall be for food. ³⁰Also, to every beast of the earth, to every bird of the air, and to everything that creeps on the earth, in which there is life, I have given every green herb for food"; and it was so.

How often do we pass by a beautiful flower without noticing it? Have we taken time to listen to the birds chirping? Do we take time to enjoy a sunset or sunrise? Do we notice the full moon and the half moon? Most people do not pay much attention to God's creation. Many do only when they are on vacation and aren't thinking of work or paying bills. But do you know that God created all these things just for us to enjoy?

What I appreciate most about nature are the colours. Can you imagine what it would be like if everything God created was blue? You know, He took time to create nature in different colours to make them more distinct so that we could enjoy the variety. Just look at the contrast of the yellow sun and the blue skies. It is just amazing to behold. If everything was blue, it would be hard to differentiate between the sun and the skies. In addition to that, the different colours have different shades. I learnt that there are some insects which can only see certain

Appreciate Nature

colours. That is quite interesting. To think of the details God put into creation. Apart from the colours which make nature so beautiful, think of shapes and the sizes of all the things God has created. Just look in your backyard or your community—look at the different sizes of the trees and shapes of the leaves. These examples are a few of the intricate details God put into creation.

I am blessed to live in Vancouver, British Columbia where you do not have to travel far to see the beauty of nature. The logo on vehicle license plates reads: *Beautiful British Columbia*. We seem to have it all. BC, as we usually call it, is surrounded by the Rocky Mountains, dotted with volcanic lakes, graced with the Fraser river and freshwater lakes, as well as the Pacific Ocean. We have several rainforests and even the world's smallest desert called Osoyoos. The beauty that our eyes feast on daily is a getaway destination for tourists who flock to our province annually, paying for expensive holiday packages to come and enjoy what most of us take for granted.

I have often wondered what percentage of our population take time to notice and enjoy the beautiful sceneries as they drive or walk around. We are blessed with all these natural resources to enjoy and even more than that to be thankful to God who created them. We can say thanks to God each time we see these spectacular sceneries. It will surely bless Him if we took time to do that. I have always prayed that through the beauty God has created here, people will come here and find salvation. I have heard a lot of people say they want to visit Vancouver because of the beauty of it, but beyond sightseeing, I pray that people will stop to give thanks to God for His creation.

Let's consider our senses

For us to enjoy what He created; God gave us our five senses.

Psalm 94:9 He who planted the ear, shall He not hear? He who formed the eye, shall He not see?

God gave us ears to hear the cries and sounds of the different animals and birds. We can listen to the sound of the ocean, the rushing wind, the rain, and hail. Above all these, we can hear each other's thoughts and emotions in our words. We can hear a baby cry. We can feel loved because of what we heard someone tell us. We can enjoy music which refreshes our soul. What an awesome God!

Our eyes allow us to enjoy the different things God created so that we can appreciate Him. Something can be described to us over the phone but when we have the privilege of seeing that same thing, it is more significant. Count yourself blessed that you can read this book because you have eyes to see. These are things we sometimes take for granted until something happens that makes us look back and think of how blessed we are. Thank God we can see!

God also blessed us with the sense of smell.

Genesis 27:27 And he came near and kissed him; and he smelled the smell of his clothing, and blessed him and said: "Surely, the smell of my son Is like the smell of a field Which the Lord has blessed.

Our sense of smell enables us to enjoy fragrance. We can smell the flowers, and other forms of nature such as the smell of the ocean and rainforests. Our noses have a practical role too. They help us to quickly distinguish between something that is fresh or stale so that we do not ingest harmful substances into our bodies.

Without the sense of taste, we would not enjoy food. We get to taste fruits and vegetables which are sweet and sour. We also get to enjoy savoury foods which we make out of what God originally created. We need food for our physical bodies to function. Enjoying what we eat helps us to eat well and get the nutrients we need for our bodies to function properly. Sick people are unable to eat properly because it does not taste good in their mouths. Let us remember to thank God not only before we eat a meal but after we have enjoyed it because he gave us taste buds.

John 2:9 *When the master of the feast had tasted the water that was made wine, and did not know where it came from (but the servants who had drawn the water knew), the master of the feast called the bridegroom.*

    Touching is a powerful sense that God gave us. It is the perfect way of showing affection to people we love and even to strangers. Jesus expressed his compassion and love for the people He healed by touching them or laying hands on them. God has given us this sense of touch to be able to express our innermost feelings to others just as Jesus did. In the scripture below, Jesus stretched out His hand to touch a leper who was unclean. Touching this man would have made Jesus "unclean" at that time. But Jesus used the sense of touch to express His love and compassion. We can enjoy each other and even enjoy our pets through the sense of touch. Even plants respond to touch. Plants which are touched and spoken to grow better than those which are not touched or spoken to. I have tested this myself.

Matthew 8:3 *Then Jesus put out His hand and touched him, saying, "I am willing; be cleansed." Immediately his leprosy was cleansed.*

Appreciate yourself

Psalm 139:14 *I will praise you, for I am fearfully and wonderfully made; Marvelous are Your works, And that my soul knows very well.*

We, as God's creation, must appreciate ourselves, not in a prideful manner but with a heart full of gratitude. Thank God for making you the way He made you because He had a plan in doing that. Sometimes, we do not appreciate ourselves because we are too tall, too fat, too skinny, too light skinned, too dark and the list goes on. Sometimes, with that same attitude, we turn to speak unkindly about others because they do not look a certain way. The fact is, did we create ourselves? If we did not create ourselves (and we never can), then we are speaking against God who created people.

Secondly, God created us in His own image and likeness.

Genesis 1:27 *So God created mankind in His own image, in the image of God He created them; male and female he created them.*

God created man in His image so no matter how we look, we are created in God's image. Sometimes, I hear even preachers refer to people as ugly, which is very unfortunate. Yes, some people are more attractive than others, but beauty is in the eyes of the beholder. What may look ugly to you may look beautiful to me. I personally do not think people should be criticized for how they look; instead, they must be appreciated. To me, there is something beautiful about everyone which makes them unique and outstanding from others. And it is important to highlight those things, call them out and thank God for them. Find something about the person next to you to appreciate God for instead of finding something wrong with them. If you find yourself always finding something wrong with how someone looks, it is an issue of concern—not for them but for you. That is not the Spirit of God and it should be dealt with.

Let's look at things which we can appreciate about people and be thankful to God for:

Consider the different skin colours—dark, brown, light.
Consider the different eye colours—blue, green, brown, hazel.
Consider the different hair textures and colours—woolly, straight, curly, brown, red, blonde, black, white.

These are a few of the observable characteristics of people we can be thankful for. God is big on variety, and we must learn to appreciate it and be thankful to Him.

If we understand that God intentionally created us the way we are for His pleasure, we will never be overcome with the temptation of trying to be someone else. Instead, we will appreciate ourselves and appreciate each other and be thankful. I have three children and though there is some resemblance, they are all different in looks and that is awesome. When we understand that God intentionally created us for His pleasure, we will not think of ourselves as less or better than someone else. In fact, this lack of understanding is part of the root cause of racism, which unfortunately is still prevalent in the 21st century.

One fact that also amazes me is the fact that no fingerprints are the same. This is a confirmation that we are all uniquely made. God took time to knit us in the womb so that we would come out as an original. Our fingerprints are personal serial numbers that cannot be replicated by anyone or anything else in all of creation. This makes us stand out. We must celebrate our uniqueness. It is something to be excited about.

God also sustains the things He has created

God sustains nature, and we must be thankful for that. How do the organs in your body know what to do? Who put together the cells in your brain to make it function the way it does? Where is your next breath coming from? What will happen if the wild animals left the forests and wandered into town? Consider the times and the seasons. If it begins to snow in summer, all the summer crops would be destroyed. What keeps the sun burning? What will happen if the sea overflows it banks?

Below is an except from Psalm 104 which is a masterpiece of the awesomeness of God. It should give us reasons to be thankful. I encourage you to take the time to read this slowly and meditate on each verse to see what God has done.

Psalm 104:1–30 *¹Bless the Lord, O my soul! O Lord my God, You are very great; you are clothed with honour and majesty.*

² Who cover Yourself with light as with a garment: who stretch out the heavens like a curtain:
³ He lays the beams of His upper chambers in the waters, Who makes the clouds His chariot, Who walks on the wings of the wind,
⁴ Who makes His angels spirits, His ministers a flame of fire:
⁵ You who laid the foundations of the earth, so that it should not be moved ever.
⁶ You covered it with the deep as with a garment; The waters stood above the mountains.
⁷ At Your rebuke they fled; At the voice of Your thunder they hasted away.
⁸ They went up over the mountains; They went down into the valleys, To the place which You founded for them.
⁹ You have set a boundary that they may not pass over, That they may not return to cover the earth.
¹⁰ He sends the springs into the valleys; They flow among the hills.
¹¹ They give drink to every beast of the field; The wild donkeys quench their thirst.

Appreciate Nature

¹² By them the birds of the heaven have their home; They sing among the branches.

¹³ He waters the hills from His upper chambers: The earth is satisfied with the fruit of Your works.

¹⁴ He causes the grass to grow for the cattle, And vegetation for the service of man, That he may bring forth food from the earth,

¹⁵ And wine that makes glad the heart of man, Oil to make his face shine, and bread which strengthens man's heart.

¹⁶ The trees of the Lord are full of sap; The cedars of Lebanon which He planted.

¹⁷ Where the birds make their nests; The stork has her home in the fir trees.

¹⁸ The high hills are for the wild goats; the cliffs are a refuge for the rock badgers.

¹⁹ He appointed the moon for seasons; The sun knows it's going down.

²⁰ You make darkness, and it is night, In which all the beasts of the forest creep about.

²¹ The young lions roar after their prey, And seek their food from God.

²² When the sun rises, they gather together And lie down in their dens.

²³ Man goes out to his work And to his labour until the evening.

²⁴ O Lord, how manifold are Your works! In wisdom You have made them all. The earth is full of your possessions—

²⁵ This great and wide sea, In which are innumerable teeming things, Living things both small and great.

²⁶ There the ships sail about; There is that Leviathan Which you have made to play there.

²⁷ These all wait for You, That you may give them their food in due season.

²⁸ What You give them they gather in; You open Your hand, they are filled with good.

²⁹ *You hide Your face, they are troubled; You take away their breath, they die and return to their dust.*
³⁰ *You send forth Your spirit, they are created; And You renew the face of the earth.*

The above scriptures reveal to us how God has planned out everything in advance and how He sustains that plan to ensure that life goes on as it should. I think it takes a lot of faith and effort to believe that life can happen without an ultimate power behind it. In Vancouver, we have driverless trains, but of course, we all know that there are people in the sky train control room ensuring that the trains run as they should and thank God they are there. In the same way, God has made the things we see as proof that He exists.

Romans 1:20 *For the invisible things of him from the creation of the world are clearly seen, being understood by the things that are made, even his eternal power and Godhead; so that they are without excuse.*

There are benefits to appreciating nature. There is a growing number of studies which put forth the argument that nature promotes health and happiness. A study was conducted by the University of Derby and The Wildlife Trusts to try and measure the impact of "30 Days Wild" campaign, a challenge for people to do something in the wild for thirty consecutive days. The results confirmed that "there was a scientifically significant increase in people's health, happiness, and active behaviours such as feeding birds and planting flowers for bees." Though there is general knowledge that nature has a positive effect on people, this research confirmed the need for the interaction between man and nature. (Coles)

I tend to agree with the above research because whenever I go anywhere to enjoy nature such as the beach, waterfall, park, forest etc. the people I see always seem to be relaxed. They are either laughing or observing nature and smiling. They are usually just in awe of the beauty of nature. How can you watch the waves and not be in awe?

When life feels like a struggle, just take a walk in your neighbourhood and begin to consciously look at nature and you will find a reason to give thanks to God. Watch the birds find food on asphalt streets, and ants busily finding food to store for the winter. When you consider the fact that man cannot create even a blade of grass, you will appreciate God even more. Nature provides proof of God's existence.

Darkness comes over your mind when you stop being thankful and you cut yourself off from the grace of God.

Chapter 5

HOW ABOUT YOUR TALENT?

The term talent refers to an inborn and special ability of a person to do something. God gives us different talents to enable us to fulfil our destinies in life. For a believer in Jesus, you will have to choose to use your talent to advance His Kingdom. Your talent is God's gift to you, and what you do with your talent is your gift back to God.

Everyone has been given a talent

Matthew 25:14–15 *For the Kingdom of heaven is like a man traveling to a far country, who called his own servants and delivered his goods to them. ^{15}And to one he gave five talents, to another two, and to another one, to each according to his own ability; and immediately he went on a journey.*

It is important to note that God has given everyone a talent regardless of your gender, race, education or religious background. Even people who are physically challenged have some of the most amazing talents, which when encouraged and developed, can change the lives of many. One example I can think of is Nick Vujicic. This man was born without arms and legs, yet when he discovered his talent and that God had a purpose for his life even with his physical challenge, he became a preacher of the Word of God and a motivational speaker. He has brought thousands of people to the Lord, has been used to do miracles such as the lame walking and has brought hope to many. This man has a very beautiful wife (who is not physically challenged) and they have two sons and two daughters. In some parts of the world, someone like him could have been aborted. Thank God for giving his Christian parents the courage to raise him up to fulfill his destiny.

As you think about Nick's story, no matter how people have looked down upon you or have discredited you, begin to appreciate God for your own life and for the fact that He gave you a talent. Sometimes, it is your own kinfolk who are the ones who compare you to others and tell you that you are good for nothing. However, that is a lie from the pit of hell. God does not create junk. It is lack of the knowledge of the truth that has made us believe the lies of the enemy. If you will pick up the Bible and begin to read what it says, you will know who you are and soon discover your talent. If you feel you have never been good at anything, you can pray and ask God to show you what your talent is, and He will gladly show you because He wants you to fulfill your destiny on earth.

You are God's masterpiece

Ephesians 2:10 *For we are His workmanship, created in Christ Jesus for good works, which God prepared beforehand that we should walk in them.*

This scripture is so profound as it implies that we are uniquely designed with talents which God Himself put in us to fulfill a purpose. The word "masterpiece" means a work done with extraordinary skill. So, God created each one of us exceptionally. This is something to show appreciation for and to be celebrated. To think of the fact that there is something that only we can do best is something which should excite us. To appreciate our talent and be thankful for it, we need to know what the talent is. Currently, even the corporate world is beginning to recognize the importance of identifying employees' talents and placing them in roles where they can shine and be more fulfilled while concurrently increasing productivity in the organization. Interestingly, God designed it to be this way.

Discovering your talent

Find out what you are good at. Your talent could be singing, serving, showing hospitality, a sport, arts and crafts of all kinds, writing, science, research, providing leadership, or maybe public speaking. What are the things that come naturally to you? That is, what things do you excel in though you have little training and put forth little effort into it? You may not even know your talent because you have not been given the opportunity to try it out. My son thought he had a talent for soccer until he had the opportunity to play basketball. With just a little training, he began to do better than his coaches. Since then, I don't think he has paid much attention to soccer.

Once you find out what your talent is, it produces fulfilment in your life. For me, anytime I get fulfilled using my talent, I thank God for it. Using your talent also adds value to other people's lives. In other words, using your talent brings improvement to your own life, the lives of others, and ultimately to the Kingdom of God. I never thought I would be writing a book, but I realized that when I begin to write, I receive inspiration. Sometimes, I have no idea how to begin writing on a topic, yet once I start, there is a flow. This is something I am thankful for. As the ideas to do something comes to you, stop and say thank you to God, and as you do that, more ideas will come.

Sometimes, other people may have to help us identify our talent. This will usually be someone you spend a lot of time with such as a family member, a colleague at work, or a member of your church or social club. You may be reluctant to take on a certain role at first, but the moment someone says they think you are good at this—because of what you did previously, or because of 'how you did A, I think you will be good at B'—you get encouraged to go for it. In many instances, teachers have been known to bring out the talents of their students. Through their regular interactions with the students, they begin to identify what they are good at. As they point them out and encourage the students to use the talents, they begin to develop them, and in some cases, these talents become their career.

Using our talents for the Kingdom of God

Our talents are connected to our destinies. God put the talents there because He knew we would need them to fulfil our destinies and to improve the lives of mankind.

Exodus 31:1–11 *Then the Lord spoke to Moses, saying:* ² *"See, I have called by name Bezalel the son of Uri, the son of Hur, of the tribe of Judah.* ³*And I have filled him with the Spirit of God, in wisdom, in understanding, in knowledge, and in all manner of workmanship,* ⁴*to design artistic works, to work in gold, in silver, in bronze,* ⁵*in cutting jewels for setting, in carving wood, and to work in all manner of workmanship.*
⁶ *"And I, indeed I, have appointed with him Aholiab the son of Ahisamach, of the tribe of Dan; and I have put wisdom in the hearts of all the gifted artisans, that they may make all that I have commanded you:* ⁷*the tabernacle of meeting, the ark of the Testimony and the mercy seat that is on it, and all the furniture of the tabernacle—* ⁸*the table and its utensils, the pure gold lampstand with all its utensils, the altar of incense,* ⁹*the altar of burnt offering with all its utensils, and the laver and its base—* ¹⁰*the garments of ministry, the holy garments for Aaron the priest and the garments of his sons, to minister as priests,* ¹¹*and the anointing oil and sweet incense for the holy place. According to all that I have commanded you they shall do."*

God knew the ark of the covenant was going to be built and knowing our God of excellence, He already put in the heart of Bezalel and Oholiab the talent that was required to build the ark of the covenant according to the specifications.

God knows the talents He has put in each one of us and just like Bezalel and Oholiab, He gave us those talents for a reason. He knows that as much as the talents He gives us are needed for our livelihood, He expects us to use those talents for Kingdom advancement. Bezalel and Oholiab could have used their talents for their livelihood and at the same time used their talent to advance the Kingdom of God. Each one of us should be grateful for the talent God has given us to fulfill our destinies. We should develop these talents so that we maximize our potential in influencing the world for the Kingdom of God.

For the body of Christ to function effectively, we need to use our God-given talents, but before even doing that, we need to appreciate those talents. It is great to learn new skills, but it is even better to learn to operate with the talents that we have been given by God. Someone could have a talent to teach but may disregard it and instead focus on something very different. We should understand that there is a reason God gave us those talents and the reason is to fulfill a certain purpose. Therefore, if we do not use that talent because we think it is not prestigious or will not make us much money, we will be missing out on God's purpose for our lives. There is always something unique we have been called to do and no one can do it as well as we can, but of course, if we do not do it, God can find someone else who will.

There are people who are gifted as teachers and should be impacting the lives of the children and young adults in their midst. There are people who should be teaching the Bible, but they are off doing something else. I have always believed that if we were all appreciative of our talents and were doing what

God ordained us to do (even just among believers), the world would be a much better place.

Exodus 28:2–4 *And you shall make holy garments for Aaron your brother, for glory and for beauty. ³So you shall speak to all who are gifted artisans, whom I have filled with the spirit of wisdom, that they may make Aaron's garments, to consecrate him, that he may minister to Me as priest. ⁴And these are the garments which they shall make: a breastplate, an ephod, a robe, a skillfully woven tunic, a turban, and a sash. So, they shall make holy garments for Aaron your brother and his sons, that he may minister to Me as priest.*

Again, God wanted the priests to wear specially made priestly garments, so He gave instructions to those He had filled with wisdom to make the garments the way they needed to be made. This passage clearly confirms that God gives us our talents for a reason. I can imagine how fulfilled these artisans were when they were called upon to use their talents to accomplish a task in the house of God. I can assure you that you have a talent and God needs you to use it to fulfill a need in this world and in His Kingdom.

Recently, a young Christian was able to use his talent of playing an instrument in the home of a world dictator who wanted nothing to do with God. However, this musician's skillful playing opened the door for him to play for such an audience. To that function, the musician wore his hat which had "Jesus" inscribed on it. Of course, no one could ask him to remove it. He was bold enough to talk about Jesus Christ to the two guards who were made to accompany him wherever he went. He told them his testimony about how Jesus delivered him from suicide. You see, those people had to hear about Jesus Christ, and it was the musician's God-given talent that provided the opportunity.

By appreciating our talents and growing in them, we glorify God. We will also be fulfilled, which will give us reasons to thank God.

When Moses had to go before Pharaoh, he told God he could not speak. He did not know that God had already prepared his spokesperson, who was his own brother, to speak for him.

Exodus 6:28–Exodus 7:1 *And it came to pass, on the day the Lord spoke to Moses in the land of Egypt, ^{29}that the Lord spoke to Moses, saying, "I am the Lord. Speak to Pharaoh king of Egypt all that I say to you."*

^{30} But Moses said before the Lord, "Behold, I am of uncircumcised lips, and how shall Pharaoh heed me?^{1}" So the Lord said to Moses: "See, I have made you as God to Pharaoh, and Aaron your brother shall be your prophet.

God already knew the limitations of Moses, so He had prepared Aaron. The two working together were able to achieve one of God's major agenda items, which was bringing the Israelites out of captivity. Once we know and understand why God has given us our talents, we can always be thankful because making use of those talents will bring us fulfillment.

No matter how many people use their talents to do what we can do, it is good to know that there is a role that no one can play as effectively as we can, and that should make us thankful. We were created for a purpose.

Whenever we can use our talent to serve mankind, let us pause to say thank you to God who gave us that talent. For example, if you can sing for the sick to be healed or play an instrument which draws the presence of God for people to be saved, you should be thankful. If you acknowledge that God gave you the talent, you will want to use it for His glory.

John 15:5 *I am the vine, you are the branches. He who abides in Me, and I in him, bears much fruit; for without Me you can do nothing.*

Spiritual Gifts

Our gifts and talents go together to enable us to fulfill our assignment or destiny on this earth. Talents are given by God at birth while spiritual gifts are given by the Holy Spirit after we become born-again. God gives us spiritual gifts when we become born-again because they are supernatural. Spiritual gifts are determined by God. Gifts have to be exercised, and they can only happen when a believer stays spiritually healthy and is growing in the grace of God. You may be a talented public speaker; however, you need to be anointed by God to preach, so you can use your talent and your gift to serve in God's Kingdom.

Proverbs 18:16 *A man's gift makes room for him And brings him before great men.*

So regardless of what your gift is, if you celebrate it and use it, you will be blessed. You may start small but as you are diligent in using it, God will bring you before great people and that is where your greatness also begins.

Ephesians 4:7–13 *But to each one of us grace was given according to the measure of Christ's gift. ⁸Therefore He says: "When He ascended on high, He led captivity captive, And gave gifts to men." ⁹(Now this, "He ascended"—what does it mean but that He also first descended into the lower parts of the earth? ¹⁰He who descended is also the One who ascended far above all the heavens, that He might fill all things.) ¹¹And He Himself gave some to be apostles, some prophets, some evangelists, and some pastors and teachers, ¹²for the equipping of the saints for the work of ministry, for the edifying of the body of Christ, ¹³till we all come to the unity of the faith and of the knowledge of the Son of God, to a perfect man, to the measure of the stature of the fullness of Christ;*

We should be thankful for the five-fold ministry gifts that God has given the body of Christ. When all these gifts are manifesting in a church, it will thrive.

Some people are reluctant to use their gifts because of what they think others will say about them. Others are reluctant because they would prefer another gift. God knows we cannot all be prophets or teachers. Some need to be teachers, and others need to be apostles. God also strategically leads us to be members of a church because of the way He distributes the gifts so that each church can benefit from each of these gifts. Each one of these ministry gifts is critically important and when they are absent, the church suffers. Sometimes, the pastor, who should be nurturing the flock, tries to forcefully manifest all these gifts and it does not work well. When we are blessed by the ministry of any spiritual gift, we should let the individuals know and encourage them.

I had my first daughter through a prophetic word. I really wanted to have a daughter. I just enjoyed little girls. One day, I walked into a small church which was meeting in a classroom then (I mention this because God can show up anywhere). There was a visiting prophet ministering that day. During the ministration he called me and said, "God says you should ask Him whatever you want." Wow, that was a blank cheque. Right away I said, "I want to have a daughter." I already had a son. God did exactly what I asked for.

It may surprise you, but He actually woke me up one November night and said, "Make the baby now." So I woke my husband up. Exactly nine months after, I had my beautiful baby girl. I share this as a testimony to the glory of God but more importantly, for the gift of prophesy that God used. The prophet spoke the word and faith arose in me. I saw it come to pass just as he had spoken it.

1 Corinthians 12:27–31 *Now you are the body of Christ, and members individually. ²⁸And God has appointed these in the church: first apostles, second prophets, third teachers, after that miracles, then gifts of healings, helps, administrations, varieties of tongues. ²⁹Are all apostles? Are all prophets? Are all teachers? Are all workers of miracles? ³⁰Do all have gifts of healings? Do all speak with tongues? Do all interpret? ³¹But earnestly desire the best gifts. And yet I show you a more excellent way.*

The above scriptures outline more gifts which God gives the body of Christ to make it complete. I always enjoy a service when I see all the gifts that the Bible talks about being manifested—where there is no jostling or envying but where each person knows their role and plays it with joy and humility. I am blessed to belong to a church where the pastor gives room and encourages people to serve in their various gifting.

The individuals with the gifts should not be perfect for us to appreciate them. When we start operating in our giftings, we may make some mistakes because we are not mature yet, so we must make room for people to make mistakes. We must allow them to grow. We should not gossip about them and make them feel bad. We are supposed to build each other up and not tear each other down. It is also good to send notes to our pastors and church leaders from time to time about a message they preached that touched us or changed our hearts. They need as much encouragement as the congregation. The enemy sometimes plays on people's minds and could let them feel unworthy. Therefore, that little note of encouragement could let someone who is ready to throw in the towel change their minds.

1 Thessalonians 5:11 *Therefore encourage one another and build each other up, just as in fact you are doing (NIV)*

Our talents and gifts manifest daily in our lives. Anytime we get credit for anything we have done, let us pause to give thanks and appreciation back to God, the giver of every good thing.

Chapter 6

LOOK OUT FOR THE GOOD IN OTHERS

As we are God's creation and God's workmanship, everyone has something good in them. There is a potential for greatness in each one of us because we are all created in the image and likeness of God. Regardless of our social status, health condition or financial status, there is greatness in us. It is important to look out for the good in others because it gives us a reason to appreciate them, be thankful to God for their lives, and the contribution they bring to society and the Kingdom of God.

God called out the greatness in people. If God did that, then we as His representatives, ought to be doing the same. In today's world, it is common to hear people say mean things about themselves such as "I am so stupid" or "I am so dumb" when they miss something or make a mistake, but a mistake does not define who we are. It is the Word of God which defines who we are. If we do not see the greatness of God in us, it will be difficult to appreciate it in other people.

God sees us as He created us to be. When we begin to see as God sees, that is with the eyes of Jesus, we will see the good in others and call it out. Many people are downcast because they have lost their identity. They see themselves as the world defines them or as social media defines them. We could be the difference that helps people to see beyond the veil that has blinded them, especially for the young people who are looking for direction.

I would like to share some instances in the Bible where we see God calling out the greatness in people. Let's first look at Gideon:

Judges 6:11–12 Now the Angel of the Lord came and sat under the terebinth tree which was in Ophrah, which belonged to Joash the Abiezrite, while his son Gideon threshed wheat in the winepress, in order to hide it from the Midianites. ¹²And the Angel of the Lord appeared to him, and said to him, "The Lord is with you, you mighty man of valor!"

And how did Gideon respond when he heard those words of greatness?

Judges 6:15 So he said to Him, "O my Lord, how can I save Israel? Indeed, my clan is the weakest in Manasseh, and I am the least in my father's house."

Gideon saw himself as weak and incapable, but God saw him as a mighty man of valor, and he was. The circumstances surrounding him were daunting but that did not define or change who he was. The mighty man in him which was really who he was had to be called out so that he would begin to think in that direction. He was a mighty warrior who had the potential to destroy the idols of false gods in his father's house and deliver Israel from the Midianites.

In the same way, after Jesus resurrected, He had to call the disciples' attention back to their purpose on earth since they had become disheartened.

John 21:1–6 After these things Jesus showed Himself again to the disciples at the Sea of Tiberias, and in this way He showed Himself: ²Simon Peter, Thomas called the Twin, Nathanael of

Cana in Galilee, the sons of Zebedee, and two others of His disciples were together. ³Simon Peter said to them, "I am going fishing."
They said to him, "We are going with you also." They went out and immediately got into the boat, and that night they caught nothing. ⁴But when the morning had now come, Jesus stood on the shore; yet the disciples did not know that it was Jesus. ⁵Then Jesus said to them, "Children, have you any food?"

They answered Him, "No." ⁶And He said to them, "Cast the net on the right side of the boat, and you will find some." So they cast, and now they were not able to draw it in because of the multitude of fish.

After Jesus died, the disciples returned to their lives of fishing. However, they were the ones who were supposed to carry out the mandate of preaching the gospel of Jesus Christ. Interestingly, they caught nothing while fishing. They returned to fishing because it was their old trade, and they knew they were capable of doing it. Jesus appeared to them and encouraged them with the miracle to prove that He was still with them. He wanted to remind them that they could fulfill the mandate on their lives. As a result of their encounter with Jesus, the disciples sent the gospel to the world.

Before Saul was anointed King of Israel, he met with the prophet Samuel. God had already told Samuel that Saul was going to be King of Israel. When he mentioned this to Saul, Saul began talking about his background and all the reasons why he was unqualified for the appointment. Samuel announced:

1 Samuel 9:19–21 *Samuel answered Saul and said, "I am the seer. Go up before me to the high place, for you shall eat with me today; and tomorrow I will let you go and will tell you all that is in your heart. ²⁰But as for your donkeys that were lost three days ago, do not be anxious about them, for they have been*

found. And on whom is all the desire of Israel? Is it not on you and on all your father's house?" ²¹And Saul answered and said, "Am I not a Benjamite, of the smallest of the tribes of Israel, and my family the least of all the families of the tribe of Benjamin? Why then do you speak like this to me?"

This appears to be God's way of doing things—to use the least qualified to fulfill His greatest purposes. This makes it very clear that you need God to do anything He has called you to do.

We all need to be encouraged to fulfill our destinies as our circumstances and even our mindsets could try to dictate what we can or cannot do. The enemy also tries in many ways to discourage people from fulfilling their destinies in life by getting them to focus on their weaknesses or their mistakes. He brings condemnation and makes people think that they are worth nothing in life because things did not go a certain way. One way to help such people is by encouraging them about something good they did and thanking God for their lives.

Recently, I had an opportunity to speak to someone who mentored me while I was growing up as a young Christian. This person had prayed for me when I did not know the Lord, and I believe it was through his prayers among other things that I got saved. Due to illness the past few years, this person had not been very active in the things of God and felt discouraged many times. I spoke to him and began to remind him of the things he taught me back then, how they have affected my life today, and how I have used the things I learned to positively affect other people's lives. I testified about many things in his life and thanked God for him. Immediately, I saw his eyes light up. It was as though a ray of light had been thrown on his path. I have begun to see change in the person's attitude. This person was encouraged and realized there was still more he could do in fulfilling his destiny.

Being dispirited or dismayed can easily begin to define your future if not dealt with and can result in wrong decisions. Jesus' disciples faced discouragement after His death even though He had told them what to expect.

Sometimes, people despise their talents or gifts because others look down on them. Someone may be good at serving; such people will always make sure people have what they need to be effective. An example is someone who cleans the church. If the church is not clean, the pastor will not want to stand in the mess to preach, and nobody will be in the congregation listening to the pastor preach.

In the same way, if we are a partner to a ministry by providing prayer and financial support, our gift is equally as important because the preacher cannot go around preaching without financial and prayer support. I see many ministries these days regularly thanking their partners and letting them know how important their gifts are to their ministries. It is a very good thing to do. Paul the Apostle acknowledged and thanked his partners for the gifts that supported his ministry. By doing so, he called out the good in them and encouraged them. In other words, we have to encourage others in what they do whether big or small by calling them out. This has to be intentional because they can easily be overlooked, especially with routine things.

Let's bring this to the individual level. When I started having children, I was involved in a women's ministry, and I used to take my baby with me to my meetings. However, as time went on, the Lord gave me three children, and it was difficult to take all of them with me while my husband was at work. At that time, my ministry responsibilities had increased, and God blessed me with a precious nanny called Rebecca. She was God-fearing and loved my children as her own. I always used to thank her and tell her that if it was not for her, I could not have done what God called me to do. She willingly took care of my children while I went out to do ministry.

I believe what she did was a ministry, too. To be able to facilitate the work of God is a ministry, and that person must be recognized as much as the one who stands in the pulpit to preach. The Bible talks about the ministry of helps. Every other ministry certainly needs this ministry to survive. We can only do so much by ourselves until we eventually breakdown. We can always do with some help. To me, the ministry of helps is like the neck which holds the head. The head is a very important part of the body but without the neck to hold it and turn it around, it will not be able to function. The ministry of helps has to be constantly recognized.

1 Corinthians 12:12–14 tells us:

For as the body is one and has many members, but all the members of that one body, being many, are one body, so also is Christ. ¹³For by one Spirit we were all baptized into one body— whether Jews or Greeks, whether slaves or free—and have all been made to drink into one Spirit. ¹⁴For in fact the body is not one member but many.

Therefore, if we are all different parts of the body, then God will give us different gifts. These gifts are to supply the other parts of the body with the things they need to function. When we truly understand God's design for mankind and the body of Christ, we will appreciate whatever talent and assignment God has given to us and to other people, and we will be thankful. A body without a leg is incomplete. Neither can a leg be alive by itself. Once the leg decides to go solo because the body does not appreciate it, it dies. The body is also then incomplete, and in the end, both the body and the leg lose. The body must let the leg know that it is appreciated—the role it plays as part of the body cannot be underestimated.

Similarly, it is not too much to tell people who work for us and do well how much we appreciate them. We don't have to wait until it is time for their annual review to let them know how well they are doing. People are encouraged when they know they are making a difference. It brings fulfillment. The corporate world may be doing a better job in this area than the church or the body of Christ.

Be the one who brings light into people's lives every day. I have realized that sometimes those who cause trouble in society are people who feel marginalized in some way, and they believe that the only way they can get attention is to do something outrageous. The worst culprit still has something good in them, and when you get to the root of why they behave the way they behave, you will have compassion on them.

One of the ways to let those people open up is to point out something you appreciate about them. You may have noticed they are really good at something. Once you tell them how good they are at that particular thing, they will want to do it even more. Tell them over and over again, and they will begin to listen to you. You may be able to get to the root of their problem and help them get out of it.

No person wants to feel condemned, no matter how guilty they are. Jesus did not come to condemn the world, but that through Him, we might be saved. So why should we condemn? God showed us how much He loves us, and we should love and be patient with others as He is with us. His love exposed our sinfulness and the need for a Saviour.

Bible accounts show us that whenever God visited people through angels, He always called out something good about them. May God give us eyes and hearts that see beyond the faults of people. May we become more like Him and lift people up with our words and be thankful for them.

Chapter 7

DO NOT COMPARE YOURSELF TO OTHERS

Comparing yourself to others goes hand in hand with not being thankful. It is the nature of the flesh and the nature of the world's system. The apostle Paul describes this as being unwise:

2 Corinthians 10:12 *For we dare not class ourselves or compare ourselves with those who commend themselves. But they, measuring themselves by themselves, and comparing themselves among themselves, are not wise.*

Galatians 6:4–6 *Don't compare yourself with others. Just look at your own work to see if you have done anything to be proud of. ⁵You must each accept the responsibilities that are yours. ⁶Whoever is being taught God's word should share the good things they have with the one who is teaching them.* (Easy to Read Version)

We cannot be thankful for who we are if we are busy comparing ourselves to someone else. If we compare ourselves to others, we will either underestimate or overestimate ourselves, and neither of the two is right. This will prevent us from appreciating what God is doing in our lives. In fact, we will not even recognize what He is doing, and we won't be thankful.

Comparing ourselves to others could also lead to covetousness and envy. This is a clear open door to the enemy according to the scripture from the book of James below.

James 3:14–18 *But if you have bitter envy and self-seeking in your hearts, do not boast and lie against the truth. ¹⁵This wisdom does not descend from above, but is earthly, sensual, demonic. ¹⁶For where envy and self-seeking exist, confusion and every evil thing are there. ¹⁷But the wisdom that is from above is first pure, then peaceable, gentle, willing to yield, full of mercy and good fruits, without partiality and without hypocrisy. ¹⁸Now the fruit of righteousness is sown in peace by those who make peace.*

The objective of the enemy is to lead us to make one of two conclusions: to make us feel like we are inferior so that we feel sorry for ourselves, or to make us feel superior to whoever we are comparing ourselves to, which leads to pride.

For example, you may have started out just thinking, "My classmate and I finished college at the same time, and I even placed higher than he did. How come he has been able to achieve more in life than me?" Just this thought, if not stopped, could lead you to the next step of trying to have things that the other person has. For all you know, that money may not have come from working, or he may have received that money as an inheritance or as a gift. You could end up in huge debt because of wanting to acquire things you cannot maintain and that will only be the beginning of trouble for you. One side of it is being in debt and feeling bitter toward the one you are comparing yourself to.

In addition to that, you would have opened a spiritual door for the enemy to come in and destroy you because where there is envy, "every evil thing is there." Instead of appreciating what you have, showing gratitude to God and following your passion, all kinds of evil emotions will be stirred up within you. Besides being bitter, it can lead to hatred. Meanwhile, God will keep blessing that person and adding more to his life, and the more you see increase in the person's life, the more resentment you will have. It could get to the place where you cannot even thank God for that person's life and rejoice with them. So, what started out as a mere thought ends up in a highly evil spiritual state of mind otherwise described as demonic.

Comparing yourself to others can lead to jealousy. King Saul heard the words of the song which the Israelites sang after David killed the Philistines:

1 Samuel 18:6–9 *When David returned from killing the Philistine, the women came out of all the cities of Israel, singing and dancing, to meet King Saul, playing songs of joy on timbrels. [7]The women sang as they played, and said, "Saul has killed his thousands, and David his ten thousands." [8]Then Saul became very angry. This saying did not please him. He said, "They have given David honor for ten thousands, but for me only thousands. Now what more can he have but to be king?" [9]And Saul was jealous and did not trust David from that day on.*

Though it had become obvious that David was a better warrior than Saul, the song that was sung triggered jealousy in Saul against David. So instead of focusing on his responsibility as King of Israel, he shifted his focus to David. Immediately, evil thoughts began to flow through his mind which eventually led him to try to kill David on a few occasions. The Bible says we should be careful what we hear because what we hear can corrupt our thinking. Sometimes, as careful as we are to indulge in conversations with the right people, we will still be faced with hearing negative things, even by the people we trust. We have a responsibility to filter what we hear and throw away all junk so that the enemy cannot have any foothold in our lives.

Recently, I was going through a very challenging situation. A close family friend heard about it and decided to give me a call. During our conversation, the person began to recollect the difficulties I had been through over a period. At the time, that was not what I needed to hear. I needed to hear some encouraging words of how faithful God is. After our conversation, which was right before my bedtime, I knew I needed to change my mindset so that I did not go to bed with wrong thinking. I must be honest, wrong thoughts started coming to me like "there must be something wrong with you" etc. The Holy Spirit being so kind began to remind me that in that same period, God had done a lot through me and for me. Instead of focusing on what the friend left me with, I began to focus on what God had been doing and started counting my blessings and rejoicing.

What I am trying to share here is that things we hear can trigger comparison of ourselves with others, and we should be very careful to stop it so that it does not lead to envy and jealousy, which is even deadlier. Instead, when those suggestions to look at others come to us, let us turn them around to begin to think of all that God has done and rejoice.

Since we are unique creations of God, it is dangerous to compare ourselves to others. Taking our minds off what we are supposed to be doing by trying to do what others are doing is a great distraction that the enemy uses. The enemy's goal for using comparison as a method of distraction is to keep our eyes off what we have been called to do. Once we are distracted, we will be unable to fulfill our own destinies, and therefore we cannot take dominion on earth as God wants us to do.

Unfortunately, there are men and women of God who have been distracted by comparing themselves to others. This desire to be like or to have what others have has led some to consult the occult to get fake power so that their churches will become like other churches in numerical and financial growth. It is laudable to become the best or to excel in whatever God has called us to do. In fact, we can see from 3 John 2 that it is his desire for us: *Beloved, I pray that you may prosper in all things and be in health, just as your soul prospers*

At the same time, we must be careful that our aspirations to be the best are not because we are comparing ourselves with others, but because we want to glorify God by being the best. We should have the right motive in doing what we do.

Celebrate your uniqueness

Whatever God tells you to do, He will give you the grace to do it. However, if you compare yourself to others and begin to do something because someone else is doing it, you will be using your own strength to accomplish it, and you will not be depending on His grace. It is imperative that we keep our focus on what we have been called to do so that we will not be distracted by the enemy.

Not knowing what you are called to do could also cause you to blindly follow what someone else is doing. By seeking God through His word and the voice of the Holy Spirit, you will know what your purpose is. Once you find your purpose, you will be so fulfilled that you will have no time to compare yourself with others.

Jeremiah 29:11 *For I know the thoughts that I think toward you, says the Lord, thoughts of peace and not of evil, to give you a future and a hope.*

Comparison has the tendency to steal our joy. When we compare ourselves to others, we cannot be happy with ourselves, who we are, and what we have; and therefore, we cannot be thankful. We have to accept the fact that we are not all the same, rather we are all unique. There is no one person exactly like us in everything and that should excite us. Over the years, I have grown to appreciate who God created me to be and the grace He has given me to become who I am. The fact is if I try to become someone other than who God made me to be, I will not have the grace to do what that person does, and I will end up frustrated.

I used to wonder how evangelists managed to do God's work and run their families (some preach in different places every week). They are able to do what they do because it is God who has given them the anointing to do both. That same evangelist may struggle to become an effective businessman because he does not have the grace to be a businessman. The fact that you are a successful evangelist does not qualify you to be a successful businessman if you are not called to do that. Interestingly, God could equip you to do both and be successful. It is great to admire the good in others, but we have to be careful not to compare ourselves to them. This is a tool the enemy uses to make us feel we do not measure up. It completely steals your peace and joy. Instead of following the passion God has placed inside you, you spend time working hard to become like someone else. Once we understand that we are unique, and God has a purpose for each one of us, it helps us to keep focused.

Contentment not Comparison

1 Timothy 6:6 *Now godliness with contentment is great gain.*

When you are content as a believer, you will not compare yourself to others. A contented person is a grateful person. They are so fulfilled that they thrive in what they are called to do.

Sometimes, however, there may be delays in our lives which could make us compare ourselves to others around us. In the scriptures, Abraham, Moses and Joseph all had completely different destinies: Abraham waited for his promised son for twenty-five years after God made the promise to him; Moses was eighty years old when he was sent by God to deliver the children of Israel from Egypt; and Joseph stayed in prison for thirteen years before he saw his family bow down to him as God had shown him in a dream. These three heroes of faith knew and understood their assignments. They remained focused. They were content with God's plan for their lives. If they had compared themselves to their peers or people in their community, they would not have fulfilled their destinies. I am sure they were tempted like us because they had the same passions as we have. However, they overcame their temptations.

Abraham glorified God even though his body was as good as dead:

Romans 4:19–20 *And not being weak in faith, he did not consider his own body, already dead (since he was about a hundred years old), and the deadness of Sarah's womb.* [20]*He did not waver at the promise of God through unbelief, but was strengthened in faith, giving glory to God,*

Delay has the tendency to make us look around us instead of looking to God, and until, like Abraham, we are fully convinced of what God has said, we can easily be swayed by comparison. Let's stay in our own lanes and run our own race. If we understand that our race is different from the next person's race, we can rejoice and thank God when they are doing well, not getting jealous nor envious.

Romans 12:2 *And do not be conformed to this world, but be transformed by the renewing of your mind, that you may prove what is that good and acceptable and perfect will of God.*

The scriptures urge us not to be conformed to this world but to be transformed by the renewing of our minds. There seems to be a constant competition in the world these days, and the goal is to be better than someone else. People will slander and stab others in the back to be better than them or to get to the top of the ladder. Unfortunately, some Christians have conformed to these standards and have caused a lot of harm to themselves. They want to be like their neighbour where the grass looks greener. We are the light of the world, the Bible says, but instead of us shining for the world to see Jesus, we are comparing ourselves to the world.

In the Kingdom of God, we are urged to consider others better than ourselves—that may not sit very well with most people, but that is the Word of God.

Philippians 2:3 Let nothing be done through selfish ambition or conceit, but in lowliness of mind let each esteem others better than himself.

Of course, this is not how the world thinks. Doing things out of selfish ambition is doing things because of what is in it for me. On the other hand, God created us to complement each other and that is why we as Christians should not be in competition with each other. I need you as much as you need me. I need the gifts and talents God has placed in you so that I will be complete, and you need the gifts and talents God has placed in me. That is why in the Kingdom of God, it is service that takes us to the top and not pulling down others or trying to compete with others. That is the Kingdom principle. I believe anyone who does not serve his way to the top is not likely to last at the top. Each of us has to supply to the body of Christ what it needs so that it can function properly. The scriptures below describe exactly how this works. Paul so beautifully articulates this that you cannot miss it unless you close your eyes:

1 Corinthians 12:14–26 For in fact the body is not one member but many. [15]If the foot should say, "Because I am not a hand, I am not of the body," is it therefore not of the body? [16]And if the ear should say, "Because I am not an eye, I am not of the body," is it therefore not of the body? [17]If the whole body were an eye,

where would be the hearing? If the whole were hearing, where would be the smelling? **¹⁸***But now God has set the members, each one of them, in the body just as He pleased.* **¹⁹***And if they were all one member, where would the body be?*
²⁰*But now indeed there are many members, yet one body.* **²¹***And the eye cannot say to the hand, "I have no need of you"; nor again the head to the feet, "I have no need of you."* **²²***No, much rather, those members of the body which seem to be weaker are necessary.* **²³***And those members of the body which we think to be less honorable, on these we bestow greater honor; and our unpresentable parts have greater modesty,* **²⁴***but our presentable parts have no need. But God composed the body, having given greater honor to that part which lacks it,* **²⁵***that there should be no schism in the body, but that the members should have the same care for one another.* **²⁶***And if one member suffers, all the members suffer with it; or if one member is honored, all the members rejoice with it.*

This is why we must cherish each other and not fight each other. We must also see to it that the next person in the Kingdom does well so that they can supply what the body needs. Above all, this is why we should be thankful for each other because without my sister or my brother, I am not complete. In the Kingdom of God, we should not think "competition" but rather we should think "completion." We should think of ways we can lift each other up. I would like to refer to King Saul again here. Instead of seeing David as a threat and desiring to eliminate him, he could have taken advantage of his warrior skills and used him to win more battles for Israel. David had some skills and gifting that King Saul did not have, and the best way to have handled that was to make use of those skills for the good of the nation of Israel. As we begin to have a better perspective about people and life, we will be more blessed and grateful for the people in our lives.

God is committed to provide for what He has called us to do and not what someone else is called to do. May God help us to learn to be content and rest in Him. He will bless us with things we did not even ask for.

Hebrews 4:11 *Let us therefore be diligent to enter that rest, lest anyone fall according to the same example of disobedience.*

The reason we must labour to enter into God's rest is because the flesh contends against the spirit, and as much as we will desire not to compare ourselves to another person, the temptation will come. Sometimes, the enemy could use someone to suggest something to us which could lead us to think in that direction. We will have to fight that suggestion by giving thanks to God for what He has done and what He is doing in our lives. Once we are rested in the Lord, even when the temptation comes, we will be able to overcome it.

In conclusion, I would like to suggest that we fight the enemy's strategy of comparison by being thankful on purpose. When we know that God is for us and that His plans for us are for good, we should rest on that. Once that happens, we should begin to weed out all the lies and deception of the enemy. When the toxic thoughts come, we can stop them by declaring what God has said concerning us and thanking Him for it. For example, if someone tries to look down on you because of your race or the way you look, you can immediately declare, "Father, I thank you that I am fearfully and wonderfully made." If you say nothing and try to just disregard the thought, it will keep coming back to you and you will begin to think more and more about it; then it will start to have a negative impact on your soul. It takes effort to say this, but it is always worth the time and effort because it keeps the weeds out and makes you joyful and thankful. This is resisting the devil. The more you do this, the stronger your spirit gets. The Word of God is Spirit and it is life, so as you declare it, life is released into your soul.

Chapter 8

PRACTICE THANKFULNESS

In order to deepen our relationship with God, we will have to practice thankfulness. Thankfulness is a key ingredient in any relationship; it brings joy and energy into the relationship.

Thankfulness regulates the intensity of our relationships like the settings on a control centre. One day during a personal retreat at a retreat centre, I turned on the outside hot tub, but the lighting was so bad that I could hardly see the control knobs for massaging jets. When I figured it out, I was only able to turn it on to the first level which barely did anything to my body. The next morning, I went back, and I was able to see clearly and regulate the knobs as needed. I went to the second level and then to the highest level and at each level the movement of the water was more vigorous on my body. The Lord used that to demonstrate something to me: He taught me that the depth of my relationship with Him depends on how far I want it to go. If I turn it up, it will deepen and grow. So, our relationship level with God depends on us.

God wants a relationship with us, but He cannot force us because He has given us our will. We can decide to stay on level one or get to the highest level, but we should always know that He wishes for us to be at the highest level with Him. I share this story to emphasize the importance of practicing thankfulness. The more we do that, the deeper our relationship with God will be. We get to know what matters to Him because He reveals it to us. Our relationship with God will not be ordinary if we are thankful.

1 Thessalonians 5:18 *In everything give thanks; for this is the will of God in Christ Jesus for you.*

    The Apostle Paul and the Patriarch David are two Bible authors who wrote a lot about thanksgiving and these two are outstanding among the rest. Paul, who described himself as the least of the apostles, had the most revelation from God compared to the others. He had an exceptional intimacy with God. Though he suffered many trials, he kept encouraging believers to be thankful.

    David was equally intimate with God, and God described him as a man after His own heart. Throughout the book of Psalms, David gives us reasons to be thankful to God. He wrote extensively about God's creation and gave vivid descriptions of the things God had done and was doing. David whets our appetites to want to go deeper with God. David is indeed a lover of God. Though he committed some serious sins, he repented and quickly was restored to an intimate relationship with God. His relationship with God was very important to him.

Psalm 42:1 *As the deer pants for the water brooks, so pants my soul for You, O God.*

    David practiced thanking God and praising Him. He knew the secret of intimacy with God, and we can learn from him. The more we practice something, the better we get at it. Any sports coach or athlete will tell you that you need several hours of training to get better at a sport. It must be intentional. You cannot just dream it and lay in bed and expect things to change.

    People have become so preoccupied with themselves these days that they are ready to criticize rather than show gratitude. Most of us are quick to give thanks to others but are not that quick to give thanks to God. Saying "Thank you, Jesus!" or "Thank you, Lord" on a regular basis is a prayer. Acknowledging

God is saying, "God, I cannot do life without you. I am totally dependent on you."

Proverbs 3:5–6 *Trust in the Lord with all your heart and lean not on your own understanding;* ⁶*In all your ways acknowledge Him, and He shall direct your paths.*

Let us look at how we could practice thankfulness on a typical day. These are not intended as rules to be followed but rather examples of ways of developing our relationship with God.

Psalm 100:4 *Enter into His gates with thanksgiving,*

- Before you begin any prayer, make it a point to give thanks first, no matter what the situation is.
- The moment you wake up, say, "Thank you, Jesus" or "Thank you Lord." This is good to say before we do our devotions.
- Thank Him when He takes you safely to work or school.
- Invite Him to every meeting or class and thank Him when the meeting or class is over.
- When you do something excellent and are commended, give Him the glory. Let Him know that you owe your life to Him.
- When you find a parking spot in a busy parking lot, acknowledge Him.
- Acknowledge Him when you find a product or item for a good price.
- Acknowledge Him when He gives you an idea at work.
- Acknowledge Him when He helps you to control your emotions.
- Thank Him when someone helps you to do something.
- Give Him thanks during your sporting activities when you do something outstanding or excel in something.

- When you are tired and need to get a seat on the train, ask Him; and then when He makes a seat available for you, thank Him.
- When you make good food that your family and friends enjoy, acknowledge Him.
- When He helps you to remember something you were struggling to remember, acknowledge Him.
- When you lose something and pray before finding it, acknowledge Him.

Engaging the Holy Spirit

When I first learnt about the Holy Spirit, I was told by one of my pastors that the Holy Spirit will teach me all things and that even if a person does not know how to cook, He can teach them. That stuck with me so much that I have learnt to engage the Holy Spirit in most of the things I do. He has taught me to do many things that I had no idea about. This is the main reason why I began to give thanks to Him as I went through my day. As we do this, God becomes so involved in our day that when temptation comes, He cautions us, so it is hard to fall for it (if we listen). Even if we do fall for it, we immediately repent because of the closeness we have with Him. As I practice this, I am also filled with the joy of the Lord, and I get satisfied in Him. Sometimes, I veer off when I make myself too busy in taking a moment to say thanks throughout the day, and I immediately see the difference. I start becoming full of myself and grumpy.

When I engage the Holy Spirit as I go through my day, God helps me to see problems as opportunities and this makes me thankful. One thing I have also noticed is that when I am thankful in the day, and someone upsets me, it is easier to show them the love of God. I begin to think that they are having a bad day. How can I help them? The natural response is to get annoyed too and react in an upset manner. The Holy Spirit helps me not to do this. Because I have been in constant touch with God, fear cannot easily attach itself to me. It becomes easier to cast out fear because I am experiencing the love of God, and perfect love casts away all fear.

Staying in touch through thankfulness

When we are in a relationship with someone we love or care about, we keep in touch regularly even when we do not see each other. We surprise them with gifts and little notes. We do this because we want to maintain and sustain the relationship so that it will grow and flourish.

James 4:8 *Draw near to God and He will draw near to you. Cleanse your hands, you sinners; and purify your hearts, you double-minded*

Similarly, giving thanks to God regularly outside our scheduled prayer times is a great way of building our relationship with Him and staying in touch. It keeps the communication lines open. The scriptures say He will never leave us nor forsake us, so it is also important to say thanks to Him for being with us as He promised. By doing that, we also reassure ourselves that He is around. Most people will pray over their meals before they eat and that might be about the only time they give thanks apart from their devotion time.

When we make thanksgiving a regular practice and trouble shows up, we will be quite confident that God is with us. This is because we have been talking to Him throughout the day and acknowledging Him. As we give God thanks throughout the day, we have strong confidence in coming boldly to His throne of grace to ask for help. On the other hand, if we have not stayed in touch, the confidence level is not the same though He has not changed and still loves us.

Sharing Testimonies

Let us also share testimonies about what the Lord is doing in our lives to others whenever we can as we go through the day. It gives people a break from all the bad news that comes through the airwaves and of course helps us to overcome the enemy. Testimonies could even draw unbelievers to the Lord or bring encouragement to someone whose faith is fading.

We could use phrases like, "Thank God the business went through" or "Thank God the problem is solved." It is a way of acknowledging God before men. People freely curse at work, so we should be bold enough to say" Thank God" for something good that happened.

Matthew 10:32 *Therefore whoever confesses Me before men, him I will also confess before My Father who is in heaven.*

There was a meeting at my workplace one day, and we were told to prepare to share who our hero was and why. Immediately, I decided to tell them that Jesus is my hero and wrote down why He is my hero. I work in a typical secular environment. When I shared what I had to share, there was dead silence for about a minute which did not happen when others shared. That year, I got promoted. An opportunity came for me to fill in when my boss was absent. I boldly took some decisions which earned me recognition. Surely there is a reward for acknowledging God before men.

We spend a lot of time talking on the phone these days. If we are not careful, we can end up complaining or gossiping when we run out of things to talk about. Why don't we share testimonies of what the Lord is doing in our lives instead of talking about other people? Sometimes, it may be a testimony we have shared already, but repeating it glorifies God and encourages us, the ones sharing. It also shows God how much we appreciate what He has already done. Sometimes, I tell my friends over the phone, "I know I have shared this but allow me to share it again because I need to encourage myself."

Let's thank God for the progress we are making and not how far we have to go. We can either look at our current situation and see how much work we have left to finish or thank God for how much we have already accomplished. We can thank God for how much He has changed us into becoming a better person. Consider how much the Word of God has changed our character. We can hear from those whom we trust about the growth they have seen in us. We will see growth even in the midst of our maturing. We can also observe how maturely we now respond to situations to see how we are growing. I have found that it is always helpful if I speak out what God is doing, even if I say it to myself.

It is a good thing to dedicate some days or a week or month to turn all our prayer requests into thanksgiving. This means thanking Him in anticipation of what He is about to do in our lives.

Being intentional about thanksgiving

Having said all that, it is important that we also appreciate others on purpose as we go through the day. I already mentioned about looking out for the good in others. This may seem normal, but saying thanks doesn't always come easy for everyone. Let us ensure that we say thank you for even the smallest things, as that could make the difference between "I am having a good day" or not. Someone could be going through a very tough day, but our kind words of appreciation could change their perception completely. When work gets overwhelming, instead of complaining, say, "God, I thank you that I have a job." I have tried that many times and honestly, it takes away the stress. Even if something did not go so well, there is always something to say thank you for. Let's ensure that we do not pass on other people's behaviour toward us to others. For example, if you just finished talking to a rude client, make up your mind to be the most polite and appreciative customer service representative to every other customer despite your experiences in the day (we can ask the Holy Spirit to help us do that).

In our homes, we may sometimes take things for granted and may not say thanks for the little things. We may say thanks to people outside for the same things that we will not say thanks for at home. A child may take it for granted that it is the parent's responsibility to drive them to school and pick them up, so there is no need to say thanks. That is wrong. As we say thanks for things which we think is the responsibility of every parent, we will always be on that parent's mind. They will have joy doing things for us. That parent may be having a hard day too and that thank you would bring them joy and make a difference.

Sometimes, when we are in a good mood, we will say thanks, but when we are grumpy, we excuse ourselves from having to give thanks. Interestingly, what we give is what we get. The moment we say thanks when we don't feel like doing that, joy comes to us too. Something lights up in our spirit which relaxes us. The whole idea is it takes the focus off us to someone else. We are naturally self-seeking and self-centered. Stepping out to recognize what someone has done and to appreciate it helps to deal with that aspect of our human nature.

Below is an experiment conducted by a Japanese scientist, Dr. Emoto, of what a "thank you" can do to rice. The experiment, seen here in its original form, had Emoto pouring water over cooked rice in three different beakers, then labelling one "Thank you!" one "You're an idiot!" and leaving one unlabelled (the control). This experiment lasted for thirty days. The "Thank you!" rice began to ferment and gave off a "strong and pleasant aroma." The rice labelled "You are an idiot!" turned mostly black while the unlabelled rice began to rot with a green-blue colour. The conclusion was that "negligence and indifference are the absolute worst things we can do to water, rice and ourselves."

Other people tried this experiment and confirmed that it works. (Grace)

My intention for including this research here is to point out the fact that if rice in water can respond to a "thank you" and thrive, how much more will a man's soul respond to "thank you"? The next time you should say thank you to someone and neglect doing that, remember this research. Know that as insignificant as it may seem to be, it is affecting that person negatively. And if it goes on, it could result in the person feeling rejected which could lead to other worse issues such as depression. I believe you want to be that person who makes the lives of others better and not worse. Again, neglecting to say thank you or not appreciating someone in whatever way is worse than saying something mean. Most people would think saying something mean to someone is worse. Well, per the research above, it is the other way around. Put yourself in a situation where you are standing together with a group of people and someone comes around and says hello individually to everyone but you, without even acknowledging that you are there and walks away. That will feel like a slap in the face. Maybe if the person had said something unkind to you, you would know what he is thinking; but neglecting you would just make you think the worst about yourself.

Let's start the day with a heart of gratitude—gratitude that we have been given another day to live and decide to make the best of the day. We can do this by making other people feel appreciated. Sometimes, we get so busy that we do not pay attention to details like saying thank you.

When someone opens a door for us, we should not just walk through the door without acknowledging that act of kindness. Even in traffic, when someone stops for us to make a turn, we could wave to the person as a sign of thanks. When we drop something, and someone picks it up for us, we should not just take it from the person without a thank you.

Sometimes, it is the closest people to us who we take for granted, such as our family members. It is said that familiarity breeds contempt but remember that it could lead to worse things if it continues. Between husbands and wives there should be gratitude expressed when chores are done such as cooking, throwing out the garbage, cleaning the car, cleaning the house etc. We should not just assume that it is that person's responsibility so there is no need to say thanks. Saying thank you to each other as friends, colleagues, married couples, or relatives, builds relationships.

Everyone wants to feel important; appreciation is one sure way of getting that across. God is no exception. He wants our appreciation. Our saying thanks to God also builds intimacy with Him.

I will conclude by saying: let's remember to be intentional about incorporating thanksgiving to God and those around us during our day. It should be a continual part of our day and not just during our prayer time or when something big happens.

APPENDIX

A reminder of things to be thankful to God for each day:

Thank God for life
Thank God for your five senses—sight, hearing, touch, smell and taste
Thank God for a sound mind
Thank God for your health
Thank God for the things He has created—nature
Thank God for your salvation
Thank God for the Word of God
Thank God for Jesus and His blood
Thank God for the Holy Spirit
Thank God for His protection
Thank God for His grace to carry on (if you are going through some challenges)
Thank God for your family and friends
Thank God for a roof over your head
Thank God for food
Thank God for clean water
Thank God for clothes on your back
Thank God for a job or your occupation
Thank God for your church
Thank God for the body of believers—Christians
Thank God for peace (even in the mist of trouble)
Thank God for the nation in which you live (He put you there for a reason)
Thank God for His deliverance

Thank God for the specific things He did for you in the past few days (your testimonies)
Thank God for your talent
Thank God for the gift of prayer

You can add more to this list.

Put a journal on your lamp stand and before you lay down to sleep, write down something unique God did that day, then take time to thank Him.

PRAYER

I trust that this book has inspired you, but it can only be effective in your life if you have a relationship with Jesus Christ as the Lord and Savior of your life because the scripture says by your own strength you can do nothing. He is the Lord of my life and through the Holy Spirit, inspired me to write this book.

John 3:16 *For God so loved the world that he gave his only begotten son that whosoever believes in him, will not perish but have everlasting life.*

Please say the prayer below, if you want to have a relationship with Jesus Christ.

Father in heaven, I thank you that you love me.
I acknowledge that I am a sinner and I need a Savior. I repent of all my sins, please forgive me and cleanse me with the blood of Jesus Christ.
I believe with all my heart that Jesus Christ is the son of God and that He died for me and God raised Him from the dead. I believe He is alive today and through Him I have eternal life. I confess with my mouth that Jesus Christ is the Lord of my life from this day. I have eternal life and I am born-again.

Praise God you are now a child of God.

JESUS IS LORD

WORKS CITED

Coles, Jeremy. "Earth—How Nature Is Good for Our Health and Happiness." BBC, 20 Apr. 2016. www.bbc.com/earth/story/20160420-how-nature-is-good-for-our-health-and-happiness. Accessed 6 August 2020.

Emmons, Robert A. and Michael E. McCullough. "Counting Blessings Versus Burdens: An Experimental Investigation of Gratitude and Subjective Well-Being in Daily Life." *Journal of Personality and Social Psychology*, Vol. 84, No. 2, 2003. pp. 377–389.

Grace, Kathryn, et al. "30 Days of Love, Hate and Indifference: Rice and Water Experiment #1." *YayYay's Kitchen*, 23 July 2018. www.yayyayskitchen.com/2017/02/02/30-days-of-love-hate-and-indifference-rice-and-water-experiment-1/. Accessed 6 August 2020

NeuroNation. "Why You Need to Smile More." www.blog.neuronation.com/en/why-you-need-to-smile-more. Accessed 6 August 2020.

www.ingramcontent.com/pod-product-compliance
Lightning Source LLC
LaVergne TN
LVHW011719060526
838200LV00051B/2962